Dear Wendy,,

they copied us!,

Between Friends: A Year of Letters

Love,

Merry

Easter.

In memory of our mothers

Rebecca Zivian	Marie O'Connor
1897 – 1957	1906 – 1996

Introduction

Truth is such a rare thing, it is delightful to tell it.
—Emily Dickinson

Oonagh to Helen. Helen to Oonagh. Back and forth their correspondence flowed, every two weeks, for one year, from July 8, 2001, to July 23, 2002. Eight to ten pages each time, handwritten. Mailed or hand delivered. Friend to friend, writing freely and truthfully about their lives. Oonagh usually wrote from her place at the kitchen table with a view of her backyard and beyond to the tennis courts and the Ottawa River. Helen wrote many of her letters from her comfortable armchair looking out the picture window at shrubs and trees, downtown Ottawa in the distance. They live in the same city, Ottawa, the capital city of Canada, in the province of Ontario. I write this introduction knowing that you will enjoy this intimate book of letters and will tell your friends about it. You may be inspired to do some letter writing, too.

I first met Helen Levine in Winnipeg in January 1982. Until recently, I had met Oonagh Berry only briefly once. Two years ago, soon after we moved to Ottawa, Helen and I went out for lunch to a well-known vegetarian restaurant. I remember meeting Oonagh then. I recall seeing how enthusiastic she was about unexpectedly meeting Helen. Oonagh, like Helen, was attractive,

and also vivacious. I learned that day that Oonagh was planning an eightieth birthday celebration for Helen with a small group of friends who would have tea at the Château Laurier Hotel in downtown Ottawa. Helen was presented with a portrait of herself by the artist Esther Schvan. It is now prominently displayed on the dining room wall in Helen's home.

Later, Helen would have her photo taken with another group of friends at the Famous Five statue on Parliament Hill. In 1989, Helen was awarded the Governor General's Award in Commemoration of the Persons Case. The Awards recognize outstanding contributions by women to improving the status of women in Canada.

Oonagh Berry was born in 1938 in Dublin and grew up there. She was the eldest of four. When she left school, she had a variety of jobs in Ireland, England and France. She married Edwin Berry in England, had two sons, Niall and Paul, and a daughter, Helen. They immigrated to Canada in 1968. Oonagh continued her education and work in the health field until she retired in 2002. She was a teacher of handicapped children for many years. Then she became a counsellor in addictions, working for thirty years at the Rideauwood Institute and at Amethyst Women's Addiction Centre in Ottawa. She has acted in many amateur productions, the most memorable one being Kate in *Dancing at Lughnasa* by Brian Friel.

Helen was born in Ottawa, in October 1923, to Rebecca and Isaac Zivian, the middle child of three. She has lived all her life in Ottawa and Toronto. Helen has publicly and privately defined herself as a feminist for thirty or more years. Feminism is at the core of her being. She is a secular Jew, a conscious and

concerned member of her minority group. As a professional social worker and teacher and as a psychiatric patient, mother and aging woman, she has spoken and written from personal experience on both sides of the desk. Helen taught women's studies at the Carleton University School of Social Work. After retirement in 1988, she was a feminist counsellor and a board member of Amethyst Women's Addiction Centre, Ottawa. Helen almost always speaks and writes from a personal and political perspective.

Both Oonagh and Helen are gifted speakers and storytellers. In the early 1980s, I recall Helen speaking to a large audience at the conference "Perspectives on Women in the 1980s" where we first met. Helen had thick white hair and black-framed glasses then, and they remain her trademark now. She enjoys the familiar, like the coat with the hood she wore for years, and wrote about in "My Cotton Blue/Mauve Coat" in *Spider Women: A Tapestry of Creativity and Healing* which I co-edited with Carol Rose (J. Gordon Shillingford Publishing, Winnipeg, 1999, pages 171-72).

Oonagh may not be as well known as Helen for her feminist or humanist politics, but she is also strong-minded, expressive, and an activist about matters of rights, justice, and equality. She speaks and writes from a more personal perspective, telling us interesting stories about herself and the lives of women, and of men, like her grandfather. We learn more about Oonagh through her personal stories and her letters to Helen. As a child, Oonagh wrote plays for her brothers and his friends and herself to perform for the neighbourhood. She has many ideas for writing, and there are more in the works. "A Homage to Ned: Memories of a Grandfather" recently won a City of

Ottawa competition. "Old Friend" in *Books Ireland*, October 2000, tells the story in poetry of Oonagh reconnecting with a friend after many years.

From Oonagh's description, I picture her mother, at sixty-three, making the trip from Ireland to England to start a new life. When I think of Helen's mother, I picture her from Helen's description, comfortably writing letters on hotel stationary in the Château Laurier or at the Carnegie Library in Ottawa, where she periodically sought refuge from home.

Oonagh and Helen have reshaped their lives a number of times. The past year has been particularly challenging for Helen, now eighty-one, as she copes with the process of aging and its impact on her health and activities. Helen and Oonagh have both enjoyed singing and a variety of sports and the feeling of well-being that comes from being physically active. Both played tennis, Oonagh still does. Helen particularly loved cycling. Oonagh climbs mountains whenever she can. She jogs too. Her many interests include travel, reading, listening to music, dancing, singing, going to films, and relaxing and having fun.

Oonagh lives in a comfortable home in Ottawa with her husband, poet Christopher Levenson. She has two grandchildren, Aaron and Rachel, who are the "apples of her eye." Helen has been married for fifty-eight years to Gilbert (Gil) Levine, an energetic tennis playing retiree. They have three grandchildren and two daughters, Tamara and Karen. Tamara (her parents have always called her Ruthie) is the coordinator of workplace literacy at Canadian Labour Congress, Ottawa, is married to Larry Katz and has two children, Rachel and Daniel. Karen Levine, CBC producer and the author of the best-selling children's

book *Hana's Suitcase*, lives in Toronto with her partner, Michael Enright, and ten-year-old son, Gabriel.

Helen was seventy-seven and retired when she wrote her first letter in this series. Oonagh was sixty-three years old and still working at Amethyst Women's Addiction Centre in Ottawa as a counsellor when she began the letters to Helen. Oonagh and Helen met when Helen was a professor at the School of Social Work, Carleton University, and Oonagh was on the staff of Amethyst. Helen had some responsibilities for social-work students in their field placements at Amethyst. Gradually, through the Amethyst connection, Oonagh and Helen came to know and respect each other. One year, when Oonagh was going through a difficult time at work, she, Helen, and another woman, Shirley, met for breakfast weekly as a support for Oonagh. Over the years, Oonagh and Helen met regularly for conversation and lunch. They telephoned each other frequently. The relationship between them grew from a connection through their work in the helping professions, to supporting Oonagh through a difficult time, to their letter-writing adventure. Mutual friends warned them that their correspondence could damage their friendship. It did not. Oonagh describes an amazing closeness, a kind of magic that developed through their letters. The writing and reading of the letters defined their lives during the year of correspondence and heightened and deepened their friendship.

Helen and Oonagh have both been writing in one form or another for years. In 1990, when I was waiting for "Swimming Upstream: Reflections of a Feminist at 66" from Helen for the book *Living the Changes* (University of Manitoba Press, Winnipeg, 1990, pages 220 - 227) Helen said she could not write an essay,

only letters. She was in that stuck place that frustrates creative people. I said, "Write me a letter" and her piece arrived, written with a black pen in Helen's flowing handwriting. Only recently have I corresponded with Oonagh, and it has been by e-mail. She is very friendly and direct, a style I appreciate. Sometimes she writes with a chuckle or with strong emotions and she can be emphatic. I look forward to an ongoing connection with her as well as with Helen beyond the completion of this book.

In their letters to each other, what did Oonagh and Helen write to each other about? Friendship, families, politics, negative (or what Helen calls "evil") thoughts, books, films, tennis, yoga, beauty, relationships, the joys, difficulties, and risks of writing, their experiences of daily living and their reactions to the traumatic events and responses to September 11, 2001. All this, and more, in *Between Friends*, an accessible, intimate book of letters.

Between Friends is a unique contemporary book that builds on a long tradition of women writing letters to each other for expression, survival, sanity, pleasure, connection, and making meaning. And to record their ordinary and extraordinary lives. The epistolary form of Life Writing "is powerful", says Helen M. Buss guest editor of a Life Writing edition of *Prairie Fire* magazine: "letters reach out from writer to correspondent with such personal specificity of audience that the reader feels like she is living inside the heads and hearts of the correspondents." (*Prairie Fire*, Autumn, 1995). For those interested in letter-writing by women, there are two other books of published letters which I would particularly like to recommend: *Selected Letters of Margaret Laurence and Adele Wiseman* (John Lennox and Ruth Panofsky, editors, University of Toronto Press, Toronto, 1997) and *Between*

Ourselves: Letters between Mothers and Daughters (Karen Payne, editor, Houghton Mifflin Company, Boston, 1983).

Today, most of us are thrilled to receive a letter from a friend by postal service, sarcastically referred to as "snail mail." What will happen to the art of letter-writing? Will it die? Will a small number of writers actively try to keep the art alive? Thanks to Margie Wolfe and her staff at Second Story Press for appreciating the significance of correspondence between Helen and Oonagh.

In person, Helen asks astute, thought-provoking questions, and Oonagh twigs our interest in her life experiences. I enjoy that about them. Oonagh and Helen will evoke your own memories and personal responses. You will likely read and reread parts, or all, of their letters, as I have done. Take the book to your book club, too, for reading and discussion.

Oonagh and Helen are unique, spirited Canadian women you will get to know through the window provided by their correspondence. They are women of depth, strength, wisdom, and beauty, living with integrity in today's fast-paced world. Open yourself to their words and hear their voices: Oonagh with her lilt of the Dublin Irish, energetically, sometimes breathlessly, writing; Helen, with a distinctly Ontario Canadian voice, acutely analyzing issues embedded in the lives of women. Personal letters to each other that we are privileged to read. Helen begins.

Joan Turner
Ottawa
June 17, 2005

What is it about letters?

Handwritten letters are losing out to e-mail these days. Postal service is now called snail mail. Kids no longer learn to spell—spell check does the trick—and handwriting is en route to becoming a lost art. So what, you say. The electronic age has arrived, computers are amazing labour- and time-saving devices. Information technology keeps us up to date. The Web and the Internet provide instant access to worldwide information. It's called progress.

Call me and my friend Oonagh Berry Luddites. Or computer resisters. Or philosophical archaeologists of the written word. Or old-fashioned, if you prefer. I'm retired, willfully computer illiterate, still thinking of a mouse as an unwelcome little nuisance at the cottage. My purity is nevertheless tainted—my husband receives e-mails for me, which does prove remarkably convenient at times.

I am seventy-eight, Oonagh is sixty-four. We have a correspondence project under way. A serious one. We send long handwritten letters (eight to nine single-spaced pages) to each other every two weeks. Without fail. We write about anything and everything—families, friendships, politics, work, "evil thoughts," joys and

sorrows, September 11 and shopping for socks. Nothing is too trivial or too serious. The emphasis is on listening and exploring, not judging or debating. Not who is right or who is wrong, or who is the more literary.

One of our guidelines—agreed on at the outset—is that neither of us is expected to respond directly to whatever the other has written. Or to questions asked, or opinions expressed. It leaves us writing freely and spontaneously. Sometimes we choose to respond. Sometimes not. In case you are imagining two sweet, gentle, aging Pollyannas, we are anything but. Oonagh grew up in Ireland, and is characteristically fiery, passionate and opinionated. I grew up in Ottawa, and after many years of trying to conform, I eventually emerged as the loud-voiced, passionate, and slightly zany woman that I am today.

We were good friends before beginning our correspondence project in July 2001. We share common ground—both steeped in the personal being political, having worked with women from an explicitly feminist perspective, having kids and husbands, being misfits and refugees from the mainstream—and both lovers of the written word.

I've been part of a small women's writing group for years. I've had essays published in anthologies, on mothering, feminist counselling and psychiatry. Oonagh has been writing short stories and poems, some of them in print within the past two years. She lives with a published poet and is much more involved than I am in the writers' community. We two are shameless hussies with big ideas—like maybe someday publishing our letters—and with a life-saving sense of humour about this joint megalomania.

We are getting to know each other extremely well via our correspondence project. Even though we've met for lunch for years now and chatted by phone in between; even though we play bridge every six weeks or so with feminist sidekicks; even though we've checked in[1] and checked out about personal and interpersonal ups and downs ad nauseam; and even though we have lots in common like friends and singing and politics and books, it's been this correspondence that has heightened our friendship immeasurably.

It may seem odd that we two friends, in the same city, both very oral, and loving rich conversation (our definition, of course) spend masses of time writing to each other. Why? We're not exactly sure ourselves. It's just that we want to write, love the medium of letters and like the idea of recording some of our stories that could or would, with only the spoken word, disappear into the ether.

Recently, a mutual friend warned us that we are risking what was once a perfectly fine friendship. We now know so much more about each other, have so much emotionally invested in our letters. We could easily become disillusioned, feel betrayed, experience unexpected, unpredictable conflict. She is right!

Oonagh and I are old enough—and hopefully wise enough—to know there is some risk. We have, over time, encountered complex relationships, lost and found connections through the years. Hopefully, this deepening friendship will thrive, rooted in basic trust and mutual need. But there are no guarantees. None. However, not to risk this experience would seem tantamount to

[1] check-in: in the women's movement, a brief personal sharing of feelings, happenings

settling for a pretty mundane existence, to dying a little each day. Even at seventy-eight and sixty-four, dreams are the stuff of life.

We've experienced great joy with our correspondence project—CP for short. Sometimes the excitement and enthusiasm is so intense that it seems childlike and ridiculous. It's not how "mature" women are supposed to behave. Frankly, Oonagh and I don't give a damn. We're continually delighted with our letters and all the surprises and stimulation that grow out of them.

Oonagh was on holidays in Spain recently with her husband. She phoned from a little village outside Barcelona to say, laughingly, that she had just mailed her letter according to our every two-week arrangement. I had done the same. My letter would be there for her in Ottawa when she returned. The fun of it all! The sheer joy of it all!

"We may never publish," I say to Oonagh. "We will, of course we will," she says obstinately, ferociously. "It's a lovely idea, the publishing," say I to myself. But published or not, I sit here smiling, writing, steeped in the smug knowledge of a long-ago dream come to life.

With handwritten letters. With pen and paper and Canada Post. With snail mail. No e-mail. No computer. No printout. Just old-fashioned handwritten letters from one friend to another. Rooted in reflections, in ideas, in trust. Carrying on a time-honoured tradition that deserves to forever endure. "A letter," wrote Emily Dickinson, "always seemed to me like immortality." Touché, Emily.

Helen Levine

Helen

July 10, 2001

My dear Oonagh,

This is my first letter to you in our new and amazing correspondence project. I have been thinking a letter in my head ever since we came to this momentous decision during lunch at the Green Door. Instead of beginning to write, I just revelled in the ideas popping in all directions and blabbed to Ruthie and Karen and Gil. I even managed to break our agreement that we would refrain from blabbing about it to anyone but partners and kids and each other. This is probably the first of many admissions to come.

Here's what happened. I got to Carleton this morning to the women's dressing room and bumped into Faith and Susan, two members of a four-woman free-fall writing group that has been going for years. Used to be five women, the fifth being Beth, who died of breast cancer two years ago. Susan is moving to Whitehorse any minute now, but I keep bumping into her after assuming she has long gone. The encounter is heightened because she is about to disappear from our lives for two to three years.

So what happens? I tell them about our correspondence and our hopes re publication. I tell Susan I'm going to use her as a con-

sultant (she agrees enthusiastically) during our group's once-a-month planned letters to her. All this in the middle of our locker space, without giving a thought to our agreement, seriously undertaken because we are both so good at oral stuff and I, in particular, prefer the effortless joy of talk (to the right person, of course) to the hard work of writing.

I want you to know I'm writing on a fresh new pad of paper with a fresh new pen taken out of a box in my desk. I do remember that I want to keep a special file of our letters and that I will make a copy of this one to mail to you. This is an uncharacteristically planful approach for me, but it feels right. The fact that you told me you had begun writing seemed to galvanize me into action. Such are my primitive, childlike responses that help to dig me out of patterns of inertia.

I want to return to our final discussion about this shared correspondence, the recent one at the Green Door. You raised the question again. I had been avoiding making a decision. We talked about why. I realized I didn't want to screw up on this great idea, that I don't trust myself as a writer. Don't meet deadlines, always last-minute effort, edit endlessly, never satisfied, not in the right mood, no inspiration, mind empty, legs aching from too much sitting, and on and on. My fear of screwing up is rooted in experience re the agony of writing when I was actually doing it and having articles or chapters published. The joy came at both the beginning and end, first the ideas and excitement, later the unbelievability of seeing my ideas or experiences in print. And knowing some people were reading the material and some people were even appreciating it.

Then there was the drought. The ideas and experiences were

still popping but going nowhere. I slipped into writing free-falls with my writing group, enjoying our wonderful, intimate check-ins; our frequent celebrations; struggling through the painful times with Beth; with my own awful depression a few years ago. Looking back, I think that my seventies have been a time of letting go, not producing or taking on challenges or pushing the energy levels. Eva, a lifelong friend, died; I ended my feminist counselling practice; my arthritic legs and feet weren't cooperating; insomnia prevailed and fatigue set in.

Despite all of the above, I was always writing letters or articles in my head. It meant a rich inner life at times, moments that burst forth like sparklers to give me temporary joy, a feeling that life was interesting and fulfilling. But there remained and remains a yearning to write and to be published. And regrets about my lack of self-discipline, my seeming inability to do the hard work.

This is my last kick at the can, Oonagh. Like the barge-and-bike trip in Holland that Gil and I went on last fall, because my biking days are almost over. I'm grateful that you raised the possibility of the correspondence project again that day. Somehow letters between us seem to be within the realm of possibility for me. May we thrive, you and I, as friends, as correspondents and perhaps, in the end, as writers.

I want to remember what else we thrashed out that day. Mainly it was around having no expectation that we would respond to the content of each other's letters. Eva and I had tried it that way and got stuck. Very important, perhaps more than we knew. You and I can write freely, unrestrained and unlimited by the other's hopes or expectations. Feels right. Agreed that we

write once every two weeks. Strange how we ended that lunch. Once we'd hashed out all the fears and possibilities it just seemed to end naturally. For both of us. Neat, don't you think, Oonagh?

I have to write about the coincidences of that Green Door lunch. That day, Gil was going through my totally disorganized box of pictures. I needed several to send to Second Story Press for their 2002 daybook, in which I will appear. I remembered there was a photo album of my sixtieth birthday party at the Carleton Faculty Club. Flipping through the pictures, I'm struck by how many friends have died in the intervening years. I hadn't realized the numbers, the losses, the endings. I come to the end of the pictures and there is a letter, in calligraphy, from my daughter Karen. Enclosed is a copy of it. Her gift is a correspondence with me, something I had always yearned for.

Karen and I never did follow through. But her letter is a reminder of how I longed to write and publish a correspondence with some very significant woman in my life. Guess you've become that very significant woman, Oonagh. Imagine!

Many long years ago I read *Dear Enemies*, a published correspondence between Solange Chaput Rolland and I think Gwethalyn Graham, between a francophone from Quebec and an anglophone from English Canada. I was utterly fascinated by the two women and the two cultures and how they exchanged experiences and ideas. I probably still have the book, will look for it in my downstairs bookcase. So you see, dear friend, this project we have undertaken has been wandering around in my unconscious for years.

Another coincidence. I check the date of our last Green Door lunch. Truly, there must be ESP or spirits moving in each

of our worlds. Karen was born on July 5; our project, sometime after conception, gets born on July 5, 2001. Strange and wonderful. Wonderful and strange.

I hope you are not bored with all the detail. If you are, you can tell me so. No expectation, just an invitation.

With love,
Helen

Oonagh

July 8, 2001

My dear Helen,

So here we go on our journey—God only knows where it's all going to lead us. My friend Kathleen sent me a card with the following quotation from Ralph Emerson. She said it reminded her of me.

> Do not go where the path may lead,
> go instead where there is no path and leave a trail.

I spent hours yesterday selecting the paper and pens I wanted to use for our correspondence, remembering my teachers at school drilling into us that personal letters should always be written on unlined paper. When I asked why, I was told that that was how it was—so here I am fifty years later still doing it, although I find it very difficult to write straight across the page. Chris doesn't know why we do it either, although he guessed it might have something to do with an adult's association with exercise books, and when we reach a certain stage in writing we shouldn't need lines to guide us. Anyway whatever the reason, my dear Helen,

you might find that you have to turn the pages sideways to read! Conditioning is such a pain when I begin questioning the reasons why I do or not do something—I could spend the rest of my life trying to work out each of my behaviours, my thinking and my feelings, and become so self-conscious that I would immobilize myself—and second-guess every move I make, and every word I say—I tend to do it too much anyway. Chris thinks women scrutinize themselves too much, and I think men don't scrutinize themselves enough.

I think in my case it has something to do with leaving Ireland not knowing who the hell I was—only knowing I was ashamed of my Irishness. I reinvented myself in England, and then again here, and gradually have tried to become the woman I think I am meant to be. I don't think that would have happened in Dublin in the '50s and '60s. It certainly didn't happen for my mother until at sixty-three years of age she packed her bags and went to live in England. She used to call England "enemy country," yet there she found the freedom to question all those beliefs she had gone along with over the years in Ireland, and in her newfound wisdom discarded most of them. The quotation that most reflects my mother's thinking in her later years is that one of Virginia Woolf's—

As a woman I have no country.
As a woman I want no country.
As a woman my country is the whole world.

She felt she had more in common with women of different cultures than she had with one Irishman! Nation-states are the

ultimate in patriarchal control! I can't believe I have just written that, Helen. Oh well, to continue on that line, I struggle constantly with the whole concept of culture and how it has been imposed on women from generation to generation, century to century. When someone says to me, "you Irish," I wonder what they mean, as most of what has been written in the past or that I have read about Irish characteristics has come from observations of the Irish male. I do not see my mother or myself reflected or, for that matter, any other Irishwoman. Sean O'Casey, the Irish playwright, managed to convey somewhat the differences in *Juno and the Paycock*, and now Irishwomen writers (fiction and non-fiction) are at last beginning to write from an Irishwoman's perspective, but cultures throughout the world are based on male definitions of the word, so I'm not too sure how far we, as women, will get, not only in Ireland but anywhere. I couldn't read Frank McCourt. It was the same old flowery bullshit that Irishmen have been writing for generations. The gift of the gab began and ended in the pubs!

Usually when I return to visit Dublin, I gravitate to those friends who have lived outside Ireland for some time, or those who are in relationships with others from a different culture. No doubt I would be a very different woman if I had married an Irishman, in that he would have had expectations of how Irishwomen should behave, whereas with both Edwin and Chris I was, and continue to be, somewhat exotic and eccentric and outside their family experience. I said once to my daughter-in-law Karin (from Sweden) that if women decide to marry, they should marry out of the culture of their families! What do you think of that, Helen? And the idea of women having cultural characteristics imposed on them? I often

wonder how it would have been for us women if we had had input into setting up our institutions—culture, family, marriage, education, etc. Methinks we might have a very different world. No borders, maybe no passports. I know, I know, I am totally unrealistic, but I find it fascinating to speculate.

Having said all that, I am now going to contradict myself by saying that when I hear a Dublin accent, either male or female, my heart misses a beat—when I see a picture of Stephens Green, O'Connell Street, Killiney Bay, the Dublin Docklands, Bray Head—I am overcome with an intense longing for that bit of land I grew up on. I do understand why Mordecai Richler came back to live in Montreal. When I visit Dublin, I spend most of my days walking around, and hopping on and off the train, which runs from Howth to Greystones. I spend hours sitting in the park outside my grandparents' house in Dun Laoghaire overlooking the harbour. The orchard where I used to climb trees and pick apples is now a public park. One day I hope I have the courage to knock on the door and ask the present owners if I could look around— let them know how much their home meant to me. I used to go there every Saturday after school—we had Saturday morning school—can you believe? My grandmother would always make me a special dinner (we had dinner at midday), and she would serve it in the sitting room on a small round table beside the fire, and we'd eat and talk and look out of the window at the gales whipping up the sea to great heights. Now, Helen, dear friend, how can I possibly grow old anywhere else? My Ma did, but there was a brief period before she died when she had a longing to return to Dublin. She decided in the end not to, but I often wonder about that.

A few weeks ago I was speaking to a man who walks his dog by the tennis courts, and he told me he grew up in Lower Town[2]. He went away for a few years but missed Lower Town so much that he had to return. The place he went to was Centretown!

Tuesday, July 10

I'm going off to work shortly. Since I've begun to write to you, dearest Helen, the rest of my life interferes with what I need to be about—writing. Last year when I wrote all those poems, everything else was put on hold—and yes, I continued to live my daily life, but so preoccupied as if I was in love!

Friday, July 13

What a disjointed letter! When Chris was in India many years ago, I used to write to him every morning for about twenty minutes and then post the letter at the end of each week. It was my way of coping with having to make coffee (he makes it every morning—the best in the world!) and sitting and drinking it on my own. We usually chat about our dreams, what our day looks like, etc. I am such a creature of habit.

I got your marvellous letter yesterday. I didn't open it until this morning. My first reaction was, Oh my God, I'm late and I'm not nearly finished—then I realized yours had arrived early, and who cares anyway. I admire so much how your letter flows, Helen, while mine is all over the place, and will no doubt continue like that for the duration of our project. Differences, eh!

What a loving letter from Karen. It seems that you were both

[2] a district in Ottawa

all ready to have a correspondence. Why didn't it happen? Mind you, I'm delighted it didn't as we probably would not be doing this together now. I do envy you so many friends and family who are truly interested in your writing. Aside from Chris, I have only told Paul (my son in Toronto) who has always taken such an interest in my writing, and other than yourself and Ann, a rather marvellous woman whom I met at Amethyst, no one else has a sustained interest. Friends and family are delighted when I get something published but are not really interested in the actual work of writing. Does that make sense? Methinks I ask too much. Anyway, Paul thought it was, and is, a terrific idea. He thinks there is a major lack of intimacy in most writing, and what we are doing is where it should be at. I forgot to mention Donna[3], who has shown great interest in my prose—she is a wonderful involved reader but I think was frightened off by my poetry. If I ever write a novel I will have her in mind when I write it.

Saturday, July 14

Bastille Day! I left off yesterday, as I had to go to the dentist, and it looks as if I'll have to go back next week again, as there is something rubbing against my tongue and cheek—makes talking and singing difficult. So, dear Helen, I am somewhat grumpy, and pissed off at my dentist, who is a charming young woman. It would be much easier if I didn't like her, but then I wouldn't have gone to her in the first place. Enough of that.

Bastille Day has good memories, as in 1959 I went to Paris to become an au pair, and was there on July 14. I danced all night in

[3] a longtime friend and colleague

the streets, and then at 6 a.m. had French onion soup in a little café in Montmartre. There were many different nationalities there, and we all sang our national anthems. "Those were the days, my friend"! By the way, do you know that on July 30, there is a meeting at the Famous Five statue encouraging women to sign a petition to change the words of our national anthem? Delete "all our sons"! I think we should do away with it altogether—have something like "Winter Wonderland" or better still "New York, New York." Bad, eh?

Helen, I am so delighted to be writing to you, and after a somewhat grumpy start today, I now feel an energy from head to toe. Now back to Paris. I stayed there for a month in a convent on Rue Murillo, very close to the Étoile. The Mother Superior thought I was a bad influence on the other girls as I refused to go to mass and was already trying out bolshie arguments at the dinner table. She allowed me to stay only because she knew my grandfather who was a pet amongst nuns throughout Europe—well, the Irish ones anyway.

I eventually got a job with a family who spent most of the year in their fourteenth-century château in a little village on the Belgian border, close to Dunkirk. I was hired to teach their daughter English! Madame de Clabsettel had learned English from an Irish nanny, so she was very partial to my accent. I had a beautiful room, with a bathroom, and my breakfast was brought to me every morning. They had a great cook, who introduced me to a world of food that I never knew existed. I spent my days with their daughter, Diane, playing, talking, rowing a boat around the moat that surrounded the château, listening to classical music with Madame when Diane was asleep, swimming

at Ostend, and visiting their relatives and friends in castles and châteaux spread over the north of France. For all of that, I didn't stay long, as I was lonely, and had just met Edwin a few months before leaving England. They were very upset when I left, although Madame kept in touch with me for years after. The last letter I had from her was when I lived in Oakville. She wrote to tell me that her six-year-old son had been shot dead by his six-year-old cousin who had opened a gun cupboard that was supposed to be locked. I did write back to her, but she didn't reply. Over the years I have thought about them, thinking maybe one day I will try to reconnect, but maybe not, as it might disturb them and open up raw memories. They were truly a very gracious family. I still have photos and some classical records that Madame bought for me. Beethoven's *"Archduke" Trio*, which she introduced me to, is one of my favourite pieces of music. Gee, I haven't thought about them for ages.

I have decided this is long enough. Please excuse all spelling mistakes, messy writing, awkward grammar, etc.

Dear Helen, this is so right. I have waited years to find someone (not just anyone, mind) to write to like this. Thank you.

With my love,
Oonagh xxx

P.S. I see Emilie Schindler, wife of Oskar, of *Schindler's List*, at ninety-four, wants to go "home" to Germany—she's homesick—has lived half a century in Argentina. My biggest fear would be just that—not going back to Dublin, and then regretting it on my deathbed!

Helen

July 16, 2001

My dear Oonagh,

You phoned today to tell me how excited you are re our CP. Your enthusiasm was contagious. I also am having a lovely quiet day at home while Gil is at the cottage. The combination has driven me to write again even though I'm not anywhere near the two-week deadline.

I have wanted, needed to write this way only a few times before in my life. Once was when I was a psychiatric patient at Homewood[4] in Guelph, in 1973. I began to keep a journal there, probably inspired by much talk of journal writing in the early days of the women's movement. Consciousness-raising groups were erupting all over North America. Abortion and women and madness were key issues that emerged as we began to break the silence about our "private" lives. And there I was, incarcerated in an institution run by men, feeling my life was in pieces, that I was finished.

I don't recall how I began, but once I was into the writing and

[4] a psychiatric hospital in Guelph, Ontario

the opening up, there was no stopping. I wrote furiously, hungrily, as though it were a lifeline, which it probably was. Gil would visit on weekends, and I would send finished notebooks home with him, out of reach of the snoopy staff. I trusted Gil a lot more than I did the "helping" professionals whom I knew would delight in further pathologizing me on the basis of written evidence of my exploding emotions. I was broken then but not completely, or I wouldn't have bothered writing. There's probably a profound but unconscious part of me that's always connected survival with the written word. And of course there's the defiant me who resists authority and in particular male authority. Surprise!

My diaries remain in some box in the storage room (second floor) at Botanica[5]. I've only looked at them twice—once when I was looking for personal material to incorporate into my first feminist article ("On Women and on One Woman"); and once again when I was involved in *Motherland* (Studio D[6] film directed by Helene Klodawsky) and needed to trigger my memory re certain happenings.

I heard an author on CBC radio today, name forgotten, who works with wood in a variety of ways including making mandolins. He spoke of his desperately unhappy growing-up years, his painful struggles with his mother. He linked his deepest sorrow with his greatest creativity, not unusual among artists. He said he remains preoccupied with the significance of family, sees working with wood and working on family as both long-lasting mediums. A neat parallel, I thought.

[5] name of condominium where Helen and Gil live

[6] the National Film Board's women's production unit

I also heard Frank McCourt (*Angela's Ashes*) on *Writers and Co.* this afternoon. He has a depth of honesty and self-awareness that is rare in men. I also adore his Irish mimicry and his Irish humour. He's touching and hilarious when he describes his father's love of Irish patriots and the hangings by the British. The father told stories of how the hanging judges would invite the patriots to say a few last words prior to sentencing. The Irish prisoners, passionate and articulate to the bitter end, would then speak for hours, thus challenging the "justice" system one last time.

It is indeed rare that I choose to spend time and energy writing to you about two men. My enemies would never believe it. So much for useless stereotypes.

I love CBC radio on Sundays. It's a gift from the gods. I would be lost without it. From the morning show with Michael to *Tapestries*, Eleanor Wachtel and *Cross Country Check-up*, I love it all. The one early morning program I want drastically changed is *Fresh Air* (six to nine), which is directed at older Canadians and almost completely dominated by men. I write a letter in my head every Sunday morning to CBC president Robert Rabinovitch asking for radical changes. In my earlier years, I used to fire off letters to the editor in all directions.

One of my motivations for writing is to record moments, experiences, ideas, connections that I would otherwise soon forget. Interesting what is forgettable and what is unforgettable. I mainly remember the tough stuff and often forget the joys, which is a pity, because there have been many happy and fulfilling times. Thank heavens my daughters are around to be our personal historians. Especially Ruthie, who has a photographic memory. They're great at filling in the gaps.

Tonight I found a big envelope of transcribed talks between me and Carol Smith. Do you remember, Oonagh, I was part of a healing circle that she established when she was diagnosed with an inoperable form of cancer. She died several years ago, had changed her name to Uma Kalyani Strong. Was a Kripalu trained massage therapist. A remarkable woman. Faith and I contemplated writing a book about Carol and about the healing circle. Obviously, we never did. Someone else is now interested in looking at the material. I become possessive of the transcripts, have mixed feelings re handing them over or sharing them with someone other than Faith. Not politically correct, not generous, not even respecting the spirit of the woman at the centre of the undertaking. She wanted her story to be told. The person who is interested was one of Carol's dearest friends.

I will consult Faith. We will undoubtedly cooperate. Feels good though to share my baser thoughts on the topic. Perhaps we will all collaborate and get the thing done. Wouldn't that be something!

July 25

I'm sure I've told you that I love your name—the sound of it, the look of it, the Irishness of it. Names are important. I like to have my name spoken. I like to be addressed by my name. All of which may seem perfectly obvious to any normal human being. Yet it's always been an issue between Gil and me. He often doesn't use my name—to which I have responded for many years, "I have a name, you know." Either that or refusing to respond at all unless addressed by name. I consider this to be a serious question, one that has to do with warmth, respect, and connectedness.

My intense response to this issue has to do with more than feminism and personal preference. It has to do with my father's ever-present bitterness towards my mother. He obliterated her by either not speaking to her at all or crushing her verbally when she had an opinion. I used to be so embarrassed, so humiliated by their battles, silent or spoken. Assumed everyone else I knew came from happy families brimming with love and goodwill. And amid it all, adored my father, who adored me, until the lights went on in my late teens.

How did I ever manage to marry someone who took years of in-service training to begin to use my name? It's kind of a depressing learning curve, don't you think? It's as though the entanglements of the nuclear family leave mothers and daughters so blinded that we daughters have a hard time learning from what is under our noses all our growing-up years.

I couldn't believe those stamps—the ones with pictures of you and me in San Miguel de Allende in Mexico—staring out at me from the white envelope with your first letter in our CP. They were delicious, making even the plain envelope part of the surprise. You have a special talent for discovering all kinds of small visual and print objects and cards. It's as though you find what is beyond the ordinary, something that speaks to me in an unusual way, leaving me stunned and delighted. And smiling like a Cheshire cat.

We talked the other day at breakfast at Nate's Restaurant about the common ground we share. Many things, many ways of being and doing. But, Oonagh, we're so different re resourcefulness, practicalities and initiatives. It took our fairly brief discussion about cellphones, the Rideau Centre, the third-floor hallway from the Bay, etc., for me to overcome my characteristic lassitude.

I did drive to the market, I did find parking, I did go to the Bay and bought badly-needed shorts, I did go to Radio Shack and looked at cellphones. Didn't buy one. But discovered that the Bay has things I've needed for ages, like a well-tailored jacket to wear to the Detroit bar mitzvah in August. It felt like discovering America. Mostly it was a reflection of how I avoid "big" and unknown, intimidated by the geography of both inside and outside. Thanks, dear friend, for your patient explanations to my childlike questions. I love the freedom to ask dumb questions, to make ridiculous comments, to miss a joke or point that everyone else seems to understand. That freedom has come with age; in earlier years, I would pretend or remain silent and feel inadequate. No more of that nonsense!

I told you about the TVO interview with the adoptive mother whose daughter hit the streets for eleven years—when she wasn't in jail—and wasn't seen or heard from for months at a time. The mother wrote letters to her daughter throughout this period, often not knowing whether the daughter received or read them. It was an act of faith, an act of love and most likely a symbol of hope. Mother and daughter were interviewed at home together, sounded warm and connected. The mother has published the letters recently, she as author, but "with" her daughter, whose name appears on the cover. I'm going to buy the book.

July 28

Here I am again, Oonagh. Reminds me of how pushy and persistent we little girls could be when we called on one another. Ringing the bell or knocking, fearful if a stern, forbidding father should answer the door, and if so, quaking but summoning up

the most polite, most subdued "Can Betty come out to play?" Joy if Betty was allowed, despair if the reply was a clipped, brusque "no." I wasn't often invited into this house across the street—the parents were Brits, restrained, very Anglo-Saxon. Betty's mother had hallucinations and was restricted to the house. Her father ran the show. God knows what went on there. We never talked about it.

Nor did we talk about my crazy family. I was constantly in danger of humiliation because there was so much open warfare. But the house, the fridge, the people inside were wide open to big or little door knockers. How incongruous it all was. Everyone was welcome to come in and share, but when arguments got noisy I ran around shutting all the windows in the house so the neighbours couldn't hear. We were the only Jews on the street in the midst of a 1930s Ottawa rife with anti-Semitism. The noise emanating from number 17 probably confirmed the stereotypes of Jews that many of our Christian neighbours harboured. Never talked about that stuff, either. We learned early to try to pretend we were "normal," to live with lies, secrets and silences (the title of Adrienne Rich's book *On Lies, Secrets and Silence: Selected Prose, 1966—1978* is so apt!).

I have to admit here that my writing is out of control. Every connection or association leads to more, and it's a bottomless pit. I need to talk about this at our next lunch.

Before I close, I want to mention how I suddenly find myself surrounded by letters in one way or another—the TVO program previously mentioned; the letters in the biography of Clementine Churchill, between her and Winston; the keeping of journals or diaries, which always feels like writing to a dear

friend; letters to and from my father who loved to write and to pontificate in flowery English prose. And now you, Oonagh, coming into my life via letters. The joy of it, the thrill of it, the fullness of it.

I think we are two Joan of Arcs rescuing this art form from an electronic nightmare. So there.

With love,
Helen

Oonagh

July 17, 2001

Dearest Helen,

I am sitting in the kitchen, hearing the faint plop of tennis balls from the nearby court, chattering kids and the noisy hum of the fridge, and I am on my own: Chris has gone up to Martha and Howard's for a few days. They have a lovely cottage in the Laurentians. I have just emptied the dead food from the fridge—mouldy potatoes, orange sauce that we had two weeks ago with some fish, green olives, which were black olives when they started a year ago. Chris keeps everything to make soup with! He still thinks there's a war on and gets pissed off when I throw things out, so I wait until he goes away. I have also gone through the cupboards and chucked out herbs of 1980 vintage and all sorts of pasta and grains, which we will never use but keep just in case. Oh, gag! The reality is that we buy a lot of frozen foods or take-out. Chris makes a chili two or three times a year, and I make a couple of stews, and macaroni cheese for Aaron[7]—he says it helps him row better, so he eats it at four-thirty in the morning! So, Helen, I am sitting here feeling very pleased with myself—

[7] my grandson, Aaron Berry

a good evening's work—and I've started another letter to you. I am eagerly awaiting your response to the personalized stamps I sent on the envelope of my letter—I do think that was such a gem of an idea, don't you? And those marvellous photos of you and me from San Miguel—just perfect! Canada Post went up a notch in my estimation. I hadn't realized they were so creative. I really enjoy writing in the kitchen. My usual place is my room, as it's quiet and private, and I curl up on my wicker chair, but there is something about live-in kitchens that I love.

Friday, July 27

Ten whole days later—can you believe it? I was so excited when I began this letter, thinking I was going to write to you at least every second day, but then I began questioning what I had written to you, wondering what you thought of it all, and as you know, by the time we had met in Nate's for breakfast, I had convinced myself that you would not want to continue a project with a woman who skipped from topic to topic. As I said to you, dearest Helen, I had felt like someone who had just fallen in love—all the joy and anxieties— she loves me, she loves me not (I even had an imaginary daisy in my hand). I wasn't sure whether you were going to come. Can you imagine, after all those years of lunches, regular, reliable, never questioning if you would be there or not, knowing you would be. And then all of a sudden I become insecure—pathetic, eh? Anyway, you arrived as usual, and within five minutes, you had dispelled all my doubts and fears—how you listened to my heart and heard every beat and understood every detail of my vulnerability. If I needed a sign that said, This

is what I should be doing at this moment in my life, I got it on Tuesday morning at Nate's. So, darling Helen, is this turning into a love letter or what? Long before we became friends, I had your phone number in my yearbook, and at the end of each year, I'd transfer the number into my new book, wondering why, as I rarely met you, except around student placements at Amethyst.[8] Then in 1991, when the shit hit the fan, you were there for me in spades, hearts, diamonds and clubs, so is it any wonder that this is happening? Dearest friend, it was written in the cards!

Sunday, July 29

I have just come in from playing tennis. It was pure heaven down there this morning, the sun shining on the river, the air fresh, the smell of just-mown grass, the birds swooping and chattering and Emma the Rottweiller, who passes us by, head held up high, ignoring all distractions on her way to finding a squirrel. Unlike the other dogs, who constantly get sidetracked by balls, children, birds, anything that moves, Emma has a mission, a passion, and nothing gets in her way. Oh, Helen, what I could learn from her. No doubt it has something to do with her name. I had thought of calling my Helen Emma after Emma Goldman, whom I have admired for a long time, then changed it to Helen, as some of the most powerful and attractive women I had ever met were called Helen.

Since returning to Dublin on a regular basis and gradually meeting more and more people, I am becoming a little more cautious, particularly with those who have never lived outside Ireland. I find a lack of directness in their communication. Saying one thing

[8] Amethyst Women's Addiction Centre, where I worked for twenty-two years

and doing another—cognitive dissonance! Oh, I do so love using words like that! On second thought, it's not that as much as thinking one thing and saying another. Then there are the snide comments such as "Who do you think you are, coming back here with your American accent, thinking you own the place?" or "coming over here and dragging up the past," etc. Friends who have returned have told me that is the most painful part of going back, and although they are delighted to have done so, they are definitely considered outsiders. I suppose, like all of us who have left our homelands, mid-Atlantic misfits. Certainly Irish people have changed, at least on the surface, since joining the EU, but I think the effects of colonization will continue for a long time yet. Many years ago, I had a discussion with my colleague Ruth Martin, originally from England. I can't remember the topic we were discussing, but her opinions were the opposite of mine. She expressed surprise at this; however, when I said that it was probably because she was from England (the colonizer) and I was from Ireland (the colonized), she agreed.

God, I do blabber on about this Irish thing, don't I? Well, I'm now going to have my shower, and go and pick up a book I won at Prime Crime on Bank Street. I went there for the first time last weekend and put my name down for a draw. I rarely win anything, so I am delighted. This writing is hard, and sending it to you without editing is harder. In his book *The Plague*, Camus writes about a man who calls himself a writer but has written only one sentence in fifteen years, which he keeps changing over and over, his reason being that he does not want to be misunderstood by the reader. I identify with him so much!

July 29, 5 p.m.

I am roaming around the house trying to find the best place to write. My room is lovely, but the wicker chair isn't that comfortable, and although we have air conditioning, it gets stuffy, so I am now back in the kitchen, having warned Chris that if he comes near me I'll scream. Not very fair, as we both love this table to write on, and he can write with me here but I can't with him. I do envy how easily he can write letters, articles, poems (although they give him the most trouble, it's mild compared with my agony). I am trying to think back over my history of writing. When I was young, ten years of age, I used to write short plays and make my brothers and their friends act in them. I was so bossy. None of my school friends lived near, so I had to make do with the boys! We'd perform in an old garage behind the house, charge the neighbours three pence for admittance, and then buy lemonade and biscuits after the show.

I did have a pen friend at one time, a boy from Birmingham in England, but as soon as he sent me a photo of himself I dropped him. Nice, eh? And then there was the pièce de résistance—so, Helen, this is a big-time confession. When I was fourteen, I thought I was very unattractive and seemed to be the only girl in the class who hadn't got a boyfriend. Having a vivid imagination I invented one and wrote marvellous love letters to myself from a boy I named Paul Farrell, who lived on the other side of Dublin. I would post them to myself and then bring them to school and read them to my friends. They were always so impressed that a boy would write such beautiful letters of longing and love. I told one of my favourite psychiatrists about them, and he laughed so hard that I thought he was going to fall

off his chair. He said I had a great ability to cope with the trials of life from a very early age! So, dearest Helen, letter writing in one way or another has been a big part of my life. And you, whom did you write to when you were very young? What about love letters? When I was in France, I used to write to Edwin every other day, and a number of years later, when we were married, I found them and felt so ashamed at having written them that I burnt them. When I told Edwin what I had done, he was furious. He told me they were not mine to burn. He was right. He told me he loved every single word I had written. I do feel sad when I think of that.

Writing stirs up my memory—it's amazing. When I was seventeen, and my brother Brian was sixteen, he was sent away to sea as a cadet in Irish Shipping (the Irish Merchant Navy, now defunct). Sailors are a long-standing family tradition. He wrote to me from all over the world, the most wonderful, loving, interesting letters. When he returned to Dublin, we would go dancing together, and I have no doubts that if we hadn't been brother and sister, we might have fallen in love. I told him that once, and he was very shocked. I am not sure why I was always so bold with my thoughts and opinions.

He doesn't speak to me anymore, which is a great sadness to me, as he is the brother I could have shared most of my childhood memories with[9]. We had very similar insights into the family history. Well, that's not quite true, as there were many incidents that happened where our recollections were opposite to each other's. We were both born in 1938, I in January and he in December.

[9] I am very happy to say we are in contact by e-mail since the letters were written.

Dearest, dearest Helen, I do have to end here, as I'll be late for work. I am finding as I become more preoccupied with our letters, I have to make sure I leave enough time for that other life of mine. Oh, to have a little wife to take care of me. I await the post like a lover these days.

With my love and delight at our ever-burgeoning friendship,

Oonagh xxx

Oonagh

July 17, 2001

Dearest Helen,

So, you grew up on Sunset Boulevard. I can't believe there is one in Ottawa. When you mentioned it before, I thought you were making some obscure connection between your family life and the movie *Sunset Boulevard*! I hope this gives you a good belly laugh. I went as far as reading up on the movie and couldn't see anything that was obvious—then a light went on, and I looked at the Ottawa map!

Your letter was marvellous. I read and reread it and delight in our similarities and our differences. Your father and mine seem to be mirror images of each other, except for the alcohol. I have always used the word *pontificate* to describe my father, and like yours, he recited poetry off by heart—Yeats, Eliot and Blake. He also wrote the most amazing letters to me, the last of which I received a few weeks before he died. He always addressed me as "Oonagh, my child"! Can you imagine. I was fifty when he died, and he still saw me as his child. I loved him for that. I hated him for the way he treated my mother, who adored him, waited on him hand and foot, and worshipped the ground he walked on.

She was such a laughing, dancing woman when she was younger, and stunningly beautiful, but she wasn't educated, so he constantly criticized her grammar, her language, her opinions, even the clothes she wore. He had a number of affairs with more sophisticated women. Yet there was a time when they were madly in love with each other. She never forgot that and delighted in telling me about it—the magic of it all! What a wonderful lover he was! How they would walk in the mountains and make love in the heather! What a great dancer he was, and how he used to buy her violets every week! In her later years she would say that the man she fell in love with had died and she was left with a monster. When I think of the shocking abuse she went through in her childhood, I am amazed and delighted that she managed to separate, for a short time anyway, the memories of that violence. When I asked her about it in later years, she replied simply, "One was love, the other rape." Nevertheless, she did live with shame and guilt for most of her life, until, in her seventies, she began to speak about it. She was always led to believe it was her fault. However, she did appear to have wonderful memories of early life with my father, which she relived again and again. In one of her more resentful moments, she told me that I had never experienced that sort of love, although I appeared to have a better life than she. I recall being shocked at her words, and yet she was right. Although I've had a few marvellous passionate affairs, I rarely took my feet off the ground for more than a month or two, and never, in the heat of passion, did I change my habitat. When Chris separated, I urged—no I insisted—that he live on his own for two years. I think part of that caution came from watching my father run rings around my mother and her putting up

with it. Although I too adored him and he me, I gradually learned not to trust him. I have a very soft spot for charming rogues, but I protect myself well, and in a way my mother protected me too. She never wanted me to have the life she had, so when Edwin came along, she told me not to let him get away, as he would always care for me. When I first showed her a photo of Chris, she said she liked the look of him, told me he was probably a bit of a rogue (true), but she thought he would always be kind. She was so right about both of them. I think I've been very lucky. I don't have those marvellous romantic memories that she had (mind you, I do have some grand memories of my own), but I also wasn't pummeled into the ground as she was. It still amazes me how she came out of it all intact. Leaving Ireland and moving to England when she was sixty-three years of age was the major turning point in her life. She had two suitcases, very little money, but a determination to make a better life for herself, which she did, becoming the feisty, opinionated, humorous woman she was always meant to become. My father was a very cultured man, intelligent, witty and charming, but in the end my mother had more wisdom in her little finger than he had with all his so-called assets. She grew old gracefully. He grew old.

Sunday, August 5

I can't believe I haven't put pen to paper since August 1. I talk to you in my head all the time, and I sometimes think I have actually written to you! I'm finding it very difficult to not reread what I've already written, but I know if I do that, I'll be tempted to edit or tear it up and start again. I'm sitting in the kitchen, the door to the balcony is open and I can hear the sound of children

playing in the park. It's as if I'm in the country, and yet have all the amenities of the city close by. Ottawa has a big place in my heart, which pisses me off, as I know that if I we ever do move, I will miss it so much. This little bit of land beside the Rideau River and the tennis courts has entered my bloodstream. (I do believe Chris has used those words in a poem—plagiarism, oops!) It's not the sea, but it's the next best thing.

Chris has gone to see the Klimt exhibition with Martha and Howard. We had a nice dinner with them last night. They are very dear old friends of Chris's, and they cherish him. I delight in seeing the three of them together, but I do sometimes feel like an outside observer, and after a few hours I want to leave them to it. I had lunch with Joan Wilcox the other day, and I told her about our letter writing. She thought it was a great idea but expressed surprise that we were hoping to publish! Do you think our friends are maybe getting a bit nervous, wondering are they going to see their names in print? I did say to her that before any-thing went into print, we (I) would be showing it to the person involved. After all, we don't want to get sued! One of Sylvia Plath's biographers sent Chris the pages he was mentioned on so that he could proofread them before they went to press. Did you know he knew her, and even took her to the theatre once? Says he doesn't remember much about it. She, Ted Hughes and Chris were at Cambridge together. It's very interesting to compare Chris's description of Sylvia with Hilary Bailey's[10]. Chris wrote that she was charming, attractive, full of life and lots of fun. Hilary wrote that she appeared depressed, always anxious and

[10] British novelist

worried and drab at times. I think Chris saw her as she was with men, and Hilary saw her as she was with women. I have a rough draft of a poem about the last few weeks of her life. She died on February 11, 1963, in Primrose Hill in London.

It was one of the coldest winters in England. Edwin and I lived in a houseboat with Niall, who was eight months old. We were extremely poor but very cozy and contented. The boat was an old harbour-maintenance craft, ten feet by thirty feet. We heated it by burning driftwood in an old black-bellied stove. Our friends, who lived in damp, cold flats, spent most of that winter thawing out their bones in our oasis. It was our first home together, and after the chaotic home life I had had in Ireland, it was pure bliss. Edwin was a quiet, thoughtful humorous man, Niall was gorgeous, and we both thought he was the most beautiful baby in the world. The boat, named the *Flamingo*, was moored on the Thames opposite Richmond Deer Park. So, my dear Helen, there I was on February 1963 with my sane man, whom my mother told me not to let go of, and there, not too far away was Sylvia with her romantic-looking princely poet whom she adored—probably in much the same way as my mother adored my father. I feel connected in a rather strange way to Sylvia Plath, and yet I had never heard of her until years after her death. I hope I can finish the poem one day.

Tuesday, August 7

Today my life is a bit chaotic, as I have to work, and we are getting our floors replaced, so have to move everything out of the main living area. I think it will look lovely when it's finished, but at the moment it's a big pain. On top of that Max, our cat, has to

be "put down." God, how I detest euphemisms—dead is dead is dead. He contracted diabetes from a drug the vet gave to him for a skin allergy. Chris will miss him sorely, as he loves animals, in fact prefers them to humans any day.

Thursday, August 9

Well, wasn't that a short little note; certainly other parts of my life interfere with what I want to be about, such as writing to you. Oh well, I might have very little to write about if that were not the case. A bit like a reporter. I find it easier to write about happenings and concrete situations rather than abstract and theoretical speculations. So, back to Max the cat. Chris held him as the vet injected whatever into his body, and within seconds he had died. He, Chris, has been very upset and sad since then. And I was handling it pretty well until our neighbour, Steve, who looked after Max whenever we went away, brought us in a bottle of wine to toast Max's life and also wrote a very loving card about his fine character. Chris and I had a very different relationship with Max. Chris cuddled him, let him sleep on his bed and generally was at his beck and call, while I made sure he had food and water and the odd treat. But I certainly wasn't into petting him, and the only time he came into my room was when he wanted to lie in the sun. Having said all that, I will miss him, just his presence. I do like a home with an animal in it. Chris has reminded me that he also fed and watered the cat!

I have just heard the news that there has been another suicide bombing in Jerusalem, and here I am writing about the death of a cat. No words can describe the horror of it all.

Sunday, August 12

Since our lunch on Thursday, dearest Helen, thoughts have been swirling around my head, mostly about my relationships with my children, Chris and my Irish family. I make all sorts of wonderful connections, and then promptly forget them before I put pen to paper. I am fascinated by how our childhood continues to affect our present. In my case, it was my father's drinking. Not his earlier years of drinking when he had a certain amount of control over his behaviour, but toward the end when he became a total slob. To this day, I can't stand being with someone who drinks beer out of the bottle instead of a glass. Can you imagine! I have given Chris a hard time over that, and he hardly drinks at all. Interesting that I am a drug and alcohol counsellor, eh? I think most of my training began in those early years. I was lucky in that my father was away for long periods during my first ten years, so between my mother and my grandparents, my brother Brian and I had a very stable home life. Unlike my sister, Eithne, and my brother, Niall, who as little children were abandoned by every adult in the family. I also was not afraid of my father and would stand up to him at a very early age. When I was seventeen, I called the police and had him chucked into jail when he tried to strangle my mother in a drunken rage. Even now I do not enjoy being in the company of people who drink too much. I dislike the unpredictability of their behaviour, and usually I either move away or do not engage in any conversation other than the most trivial of exchanges. Yet I have a lot of time and energy for those who are trying to change their lives.

I can't believe what has just happened. Aaron is at a rowing regatta in St. Catharines, and he got drunk last night and could

now end up being suspended from future regattas this year. History certainly has a way of repeating itself. When son Niall was sixteen, he got drunk and smashed some windows at a school. He had to appear in court. I can still remember the awful feeling of humiliation when the judge lectured Edwin and me over our lack of control over our son. Helen says Aaron feels so ashamed. That's good, but I hope he doesn't beat up too much on himself. After all, it's not the experience that will count in the long run, it's what he does with it. His girlfriend, Sonia, is furious with him, so all in all he's certainly getting the message that it's not "cool."

This has disrupted my writing; what a pain. Our house continues to be a total mess, as the floors are still not done. I am now going to have a shower, walk to the market and buy some birthday cards—one for my brother Niall who lives in Mallorca, and one for my old friend Dorothy Thurley. We have known each other since 1970 and have supported each other through depression, child-rearing, divorce, and all the other trials and tribulations of life.

With love, Oonagh xxx

Helen

August 7, 2001

My dear Oonagh,

I've been struggling with beginning this letter, not because there isn't lots to tell you about and not because our CP has lost its magnetism but because my deeply entrenched resistance to writing has reared its misbegotten head. It's such a terrible pattern—unless the surrounding conditions are close to perfection, I lose my drive and find other diversions. And thus walk away from what it is that I truly want to do. There are reasons, of course—aren't there always?—and at some other juncture, I'll write about them or talk with you and then write. But not right now.

And, Oonagh, please don't think this has anything to do with you and my reactions to your letter. It does not! This particular failing is mine alone, and I don't like it and I want to get beyond it and I want our CP to help me break the back of it. So tonight I am pushing against the grain, writing haltingly and somewhat unspontaneously, but nevertheless *writing*. It feels hard and it feels right. I am determined as hell to do the "work," to stick with our structure no matter what. I hope you can live with this part

48

of me and that it doesn't dilute your joy, your passion, and your scrumptious enthusiasm about our CP.

I loved your last letter. Especially the part about...

The phone just rang—Karen home from Newfoundland. She, Michael, Gabriel. They've fallen in love with the place. Were in Salvage, a tiny village of 206 people. We talked for an hour, mostly about the joys of being with plain folk, near the ocean, breathing the fresh sea air, loving the wind at nights, reading anything and everything about "the rock," happy to be far from sophisticated Toronto and the CBC.

Then the phone again—Fran is using our cottage while we're in Detroit, first time. So I had to explain all the quirky stuff. I get enormous satisfaction out of lending the place to friends. Because we seldom "entertain" and because I don't cook or bake and I have little imagination in gifts, my pleasure is to share cottage or car and even the condo (guests of downstairs neighbours).

To continue re your last letter. It was the parts about cleaning out the fridge while Christopher was away (shades of life with Gil), re Esther and the evaluation or devaluation of an old friendship (my favourite poem of yours) and how you began writing plays and made your brothers and friends act in them. I was stunned by your courage and imagination when you were fourteen and invented a romantic boyfriend from whom you "received" adoring missives. What a marvellously brazen kid you must have been! And then love letters to Edwin—I'm with him re how awful it was of you to burn them, even though sometimes I want to burn my own diaries thinking it would be a kindness to my nearest and dearest. I'm jealous of your history of writing, of your adventures and adventurousness from an early age.

My writing history is, by comparison, very conventional—people enjoyed my letters, said I wrote the way I spoke and spoke the way I wrote. Mainly, I had a correspondence with my father. He wrote beautifully, with a command of the English language that was amazing in an immigrant from Poland who arrived in Canada at age twelve. He was a real anglophile, quoted English poets like Keats, Shelley, Wordsworth, knew British history and Canadian history in remarkable detail and depth. He used to write on RCMP stationery, with pride in his position as purchasing agent. I still have some of his letters to me and from me to him (mainly from Queen's University) stashed away. I also have a series of letters he wrote to his father and some from my grandfather.

Interrupted again! Damn. Gil wants to see the news and so do I—all about the interim APEC[11] report and the gruelling heat wave across Canada. I'm connecting to our search for the right place to write, Oonagh. For me, it's the living room, always has been since my days at Carleton when I first began to write and publish. I had written a modest piece prior to Carleton about adoptive applicant groups, which I developed at Ottawa CAS (Children's Aid Society) in the 1960s. Part of my job then was to do an article describing this group project, and it was published in a skinny journal put out by the Ontario association of CAS. I was proud of that accomplishment. However, once the group project was launched—it was a part-time job on contract—I was let go by the relatively new director of the adoption department. In those days of social worker shortages, I had originally been hired to do specific parts of

[11] Asia Pacific Economic Cooperation

the adoption job—like intake and applicant groups. I was also the resident "radical" in adoption. Yet I didn't chain myself to the gallery railings of the House of Commons (abortion cavalcade) because I likely would have lost my CAS job.

Back to my father and grandfather's letters. It was a close father-son connection, but the letters were often vehicles for bitter critiques of their wives. The letters are sitting in a shoebox in my office cupboard, reflecting patterns, handed down from father to son, of thinking their lives were ruined by women. Meanwhile, they fanned the flames of anger in each of their families—kind of like an early version of the fathers' rights movement. I'm in the middle of all this as kid and adolescent, adored by my father as a sweet, attractive and non-materialistic daughter, the kind of child-woman he would, he thought, like to have married. No physical or sexual contact, but he would confide his sorrows to me, and I in turn would hate my mother for not making my wonderful father a happy man.

I never wrote to my mother and father together—letters were mainly to my father and at times to my mother. I still don't like to write to couples as couples, which of course is what nice, well brought up people do—or did. Gil never wrote me love letters. Mine to him were more endearing, more affectionate, but not love letters. I was bursting, silently, with romantic and sentimental hopes and dreams from the time I was a kid, but I was so repressed and lost growing up that the fires burned only internally.

Do you find this all hard to believe?

I used to enjoy writing letters to Ruthie and Karen when we were apart. I took pride in writing them interesting letters (my definition, maybe not theirs). Karen was quarantined at the Civic

Hospital when she was around two years old—a mix of impetigo and poison ivy—and we were not allowed to visit (imagine!). So each day I would write a little note to her and send some tiny treat or present with it, for the nurse to remind this poor little woebegone child that she was loved and not abandoned. Why on earth do we ever cooperate with doctors and hospitals and the whole damn medical establishment! P.S. She survived.

I haven't written about a few significant happenings lately. Like our amazing envisioning group get-together at Rosemary's cottage; Jan's touching story about how she gave her beloved horse to a thirteen-year-old girl who lives nearby (more on this some other time); and the let-down I often feel when I come home after spending quality time with feminists, full of rich conversation, warm responsiveness and lots of laughs.

We're having lunch tomorrow and I'm glad of that. I think our lunches in between the writing are very important. It sort of glues the pieces together in some way. I may or may not send this off as is—or do a bit more.

I wish I could be as passionate, as sparkling, as rich in feeling as you are, dear Oonagh. But this letter has been me swimming upstream, working at my writing instead of waiting for the spirit to descend, or ascend, or move me. The only thing that makes me plod uphill is my desperate wish for our CP to flourish. So bear with me, my dear friend, I am in process. For a change!

Lots of love,
Helen

Oonagh,

It's the next day and I just checked in my CP file to see the dates of my first two letters. One July 10, the next July 16. And now it's August 8. Yikes. I am delinquent. I've screwed up the timing. I have fallen into my old pattern of being unreliable, untrustworthy, and un-everything else re writing.

But wait. Watch how I wiggle out of this close shave. If I began July 10, counting every two weeks, I am—theoretically—only one day late in sending my third letter off. Ah, the sheer joy of knowing I have not fallen off the wagon by much.

I will mail my letters tonight—quick, Helen, find the envelopes, stamps, put shoes on; fast, to the mailbox before it's too dark. Good thing it's around the corner. Perchance even snail mail will fly to St. Andrew Street by Friday.

Meanwhile, I love this madness!! From your zany seventy-seven-year-old friend who has never fully grown up. I'm so grateful, Oonagh, that you and I have found one another in this new way.

Madly and lovingly,
Helen

Helen

August 22, 2001

My dear Oonagh,

I am feeling very smug. It's the day before I leave for Niagara-on-the Lake with the kids, and in typical fashion I have dealt with most of the loose ends needing attention. Mostly, I'm a great procrastinator, but when a trip is coming up, however brief, I scurry about putting things away, getting things done, organizing my life so that when I return, all is in order. It's always a joy coming home—partly because I'm a physical wreck after even a weekend away and partly because I'm returning to order and routine. I'm a creature of opposites, in so many ways—needing freedom and excitement and people on the one hand, structure, routine and silence on the other.

Lots to tell you, Oonagh. I fairly burst with my experiences and reactions these days, wanting and needing to tell you my stories. The phone no longer satisfies in this regard, though I want us to keep touching base and checking in. It's the writing and the lunches that are rich in possibilities and depth.

Some of the romance got knocked out of me over the years—including the tears that used to pour out at the least provocation.

Somehow, for good or ill (I was sometimes almost overwhelmed by my own intensity)—passion remained at the centre of me and found other forms of expression. Not accidental that I became, at different stages, committed left-winger, mother and feminist.

We talked at lunch about mutual trust, our need for each other, both elements underpinning the foundation of this experiment. Can't recall if I've written about this before (didn't copy my last letter to you). These were among the ingredients Eva and I had in our long and very important friendship—Eva (Kenyon) and I once wrote about this in an article in *Spider Woman* entitled "Revisiting a Very Old Friendship."

I've never dared to think that in my old age I would find a friend with whom I might have that kind of closeness. I've learned, over the years, to appreciate different kinds of friends with different kinds of gifts. But deep down inside me I yearn for a Damon and Pythias connection, one that binds me to a friend through thick and thin, through conflicts and disappointments, through space and time.

I have a story from childhood. My mother took me to an *Our Gang* comedy movie! I might have been seven or eight. Title— *When a Feller Needs a Friend*. Supposed to be funny. I sobbed through the whole movie (obviously the theme, not the humour, got to me). My mother was angry and embarrassed with this moody second daughter who was making a spectacle of herself in public. Said if I didn't learn to control myself, she wouldn't take me again.

Does the episode tell you something about me and friendship? And intensity and passion? At seventy-seven, I've calmed down, grown up, learned lots re human behaviour, my own and others.

I'm much more wary now, have learned to adapt to difference rather than reaching for the clouds. But like a first love affair that is never completely forgotten, the hopes and dreams of childhood remain at the core of me. I hope this doesn't scare the hell out of you. I think I've given up on finding a soul mate—adolescence really can't be repeated. But I don't think I'd be involved in our CP if I weren't still searching for a deeper connection, a deeper friendship, a sisterhood that comes closer to those hopes and dreams.

Karen just called, is meeting me at the train station in Toronto tomorrow noon. Then we drive to Niagara-on-the-Lake to meet Ruthie, who is already there. We're all thrilled to be going—mostly to be together for four days but also to see the plays. Of all the performing arts, I love theatre best (opera too, a form of theatre). Did you know that I once acted in amateur theatre in a left-wing Jewish organization in Toronto (lived there for ten years)? I loved being on stage, always did beautifully at auditions with voice, feeling and expression. But never recognized the importance of the body, the flow of movement, the authentic presence of the actor within a character in a play.

I never thought of studying theatre, or of applying to CBC for any kind of work in radio. The guys did these things. I never thought I could do anything that I really wanted to do. Like becoming a linguist or a journalist or a performer. The bar mitzvah boy in Detroit, David, who is a likeable and interesting kid, appeared to be so confident and comfortable, so fearless in coping with everybody and everything. If we girls and women had had beginnings like that, think of what we might have become and how the world could have been enriched by our contributions.

Am reading Katharine Graham's (*Washington Post*) autobiography. Totally "privileged" background, interesting parents, opportunities and connections galore. She marries Phillip Graham (he takes over *Post* from her father) and becomes the submissive, subservient wife (servants and all). He makes the decisions, she does the work; he diminishes her with his cutting "wit"; she thinks it's funny too. The kids begin to make fun of her, etc., etc., and gradually she loses complete confidence. All described in a very low-key way; no rage (he had it all). Classic example of institution of marriage disabling and destabilizing women. Fascinating background material re U.S. politics and all the known public figures past WWII and during the McCarthy period.

This letter is not what I intended, Oonagh. Was going to describe Jean and Ben's visit to our cottage—how wonderful it was to not sit around *only* discussing "politics," the men, that is. With just the four of us, and old age having alerted all of us to the importance of being who we really are, we talked of many things, swam joyously, reminisced and thoroughly enjoyed one another. When I think of the years of wasted "social" evenings mainly listening to men talk their version of politics, allowing them to set the agenda and to silence us with their imagined superiority, I could weep.

Our writing group, the three of us now left, met with Heather Menzies[12] recently to figure out how to move on. Out of the meeting, we almost decided to take a course in creative writing in the fall. But the more I thought about it, the less I liked the prospect. A mixed class (women and

[12] Canadian author and feminist

men), meets in the opposite end of city and is not a small, intimate group. I've decided not to proceed. Womansing choir will be my new involvement, and our CP takes time.

The writing course could be helpful in concrete ways. But I've never gone in that kind of straight line, pursuing a logical course to reach whatever logical ends.

Determined to get this in mail before 6 p.m. today. I'm grateful, Oonagh, that I have you as friend, feminist sidekick and adventurous writing partner.

<div style="text-align: right">

With much love,
Helen

</div>

Oonagh

Monday, August 20, 2001, 9 a.m.

Dearest Helen,

I have so neglected you this week, and in doing so, I feel I have neglected myself too! What a shitty week I've had; I don't know where to start. I'm writing now, because I don't have to be at work until noon, as there is a board meeting tonight, and I, once more, am a staff rep—more about Amethyst later.

Dearest Helen, can I relate to your struggles with writing! What is it that stops us? When I write (during that time), my words seem so pedestrian that it's as if the right side of my brain goes to sleep; the right side is the creative side, isn't it? What I have tried to do during those periods is to edit stuff that I have written over the years. It has helped, somewhat, and certainly some of my poems have benefited, but mostly I don't write for months and months, and like you, I have lots to write about, but somehow cannot pick up a pen—methinks it has something to do with depression—what do you think? And conditioning—to put family, work and household duties first; for me, this is so automatic, like a reflex action. I don't even have to think about it; I just do. A case in point is that when I walk into Amethyst, I go to the

kitchen, and instead of just grabbing a glass of water and going to my office, I put all the dirty dishes in the dishwasher, make fresh coffee, tidy the papers, etc., etc., and every time I go into the kitchen during the day, I do the same thing. I was nine when my sister, Eithne, was born, so from that early age I began my training for motherhood and caregiver, as my mother became more and more depressed and my father more and more drunk. I took over the household chores and the care of Eithne and Niall, my younger brother. When I was eleven, I missed nearly a year of school as my mother became extremely ill with rheumatic fever and was bedridden. Needless to say, I never caught up on my schoolwork. I was relieved when, because of the lack of money at home, I had to leave school at sixteen and began my training as a nurse—that didn't last long, as my dislike of authority figures and hierarchical structures was firmly in place by then, thanks to the schools I went to and the encouragement of both my parents!

I can't believe I've drifted into all this stuff. I have other things I want to write about. What a pain, and now I have to get ready for work. What a roundabout way of trying to sort out why I have so much trouble writing sometimes!

Saturday, August 25

Oh, my God, Helen, I am still struggling with this letter, and I received another one from you on Thursday. I can't tell you how relieved I am that we made a deadline of two weeks. Otherwise I would be drifting off into la-la land—meaning talking to you in my head and never getting it down on paper. It seems to me that these letters are becoming more and more about our difficulties around writing and our desperate desire to write. If we both didn't

have anything interesting to write about, it would be understandable, but we have. Helen, we have happenings, thoughts, ideas, feelings, creative thinking, etc., etc. Aside from you, dear, dear friend—doppelgänger—thoughts of my mother, packing two suitcases and leaving Ireland in her sixty-fourth year and making a new life for herself with no money, little family support, but with a gutsiness that puts anything I do in the ha'penny position. So if she can do what she did at sixty-three, there should be no reason why I can't, at sixty-three, keep on writing my letters and poetry and stories, right? I had a delicious (one of your words, Helen) little phone call with daughter Helen the other day; it went like this:

Me: The actor who played Nora in the film looked very like my mother. Did you realize how very beautiful she was?

Helen: Yes, I know she was beautiful. I have a beautiful mother too.

Me: Not as beautiful as mine was.

Helen: Rubbish. Mine is more beautiful than yours ever was. So shut up.

At this point we dissolved into hysterical laughter, and I told her of the time when I was about ten years of age, how I knocked a good friend of mine off her bike because she said that her mother was more beautiful than mine. When I told Chris, he said he thought only boys did that sort of thing when there was criticism of their fathers. About *Nora*; did you see it? If you didn't, don't bother, but read the book. I very nearly walked out after the first

twenty minutes. It had very little to do with the life of Nora and much to do with Joyce's sexual needs. What a predator he was both sexually and emotionally to her! I believe the film said more about the director, Pat Murphy, than it did about Nora. I would love to know how Brenda Maddox[13] feels about it. I have started to read the book again. I need to take the nasty taste of the film out of my head. I was a total wreck coming out of the Bytown that night and cried for hours when I got home. I know part of it was that Nora looked so like my mother and was put down intellectually and emotionally in the same way. My mother used to say she had more in common with women in Africa or India or China than she had with one Irishman. Having said all that, I loved his (Joyce's) book of short stories, *Dubliners,* and yes, I want to get a copy of Oscar Wilde's letters. I have read everything he has written. One of my favourite writers at one time; I carried a book of his essays around with me everywhere and read and reread his "De Profundis," though I'm not sure if it would have the same impact on me today.

Sunday, August 26

I'm so glad it's raining, as I had already made up my mind this morning that I was going to stay in all day and not go for a walk. Unusual for me, but I feel extremely tired today. I did play a half-assed game of tennis this morning, but it didn't do anything for me. Grump, grump, grump. I had just spoken to my sister and told her I was going over to Dublin in October for three days but will not be going down to Cork to see her. She took it

[13] author of the book, *Nora*, about the wife of James Joyce

reasonably well, but I know she is disappointed. I suggested she come up to Dublin for a day. She might do that. Unlike your sister, Helen, Eithne would love to have me living near her. I still think she sees me as her mother, as I was the one who looked after her all the time when we were both growing up. Did your sister take care of you when you were young, Helen? Like you, I have little in common with any of my family, and none of them seem at all interested in the person I have become. It seems that all we have in common is my mother's womb—have I said that before? I am always amazed when I hear of someone like Rosemary Murphy and her sisters and how much they enjoy each other's company. And your Karen and Ruthie; I don't know many people like that. My own children are not at all close to each other. I think they like each other well enough, but I would not say they are intimate. I think Helen would like to be closer to Paul, but she and Niall had difficulties with each other when they were young, and it hasn't been resolved, mainly because they are very different. Helen has great generosity of spirit, and has a wonderful laugh, which when I hear it gives me warm fuzzies. It's incredible that she and I have managed to survive our dislikes and hatreds of each other's words and actions without a major rift (well up to now anyway!). We have both hated each other's guts at times, and I think it says something about the two of us that we have managed to survive thus far, and certainly as Aaron gets older, or has got older, and becomes a young man, I do not feel he needs my support as he did when he was young, and she doesn't either. As you can see from my childhood, I was conditioned at a very early age to take care of women and children. No wonder I work at Amethyst! For years, when I

was growing up, I wanted to be a boy. I played soccer, climbed trees, did everything my brothers did. I wanted to become a sea captain—can you believe?—and was very envious that both my brothers were able to go to sea, and neither of them wanted to.

I loved your story about going to see *Our Gang* and sobbing while everyone else laughed. I did the same when I saw Charlie Chaplin's *Gold Rush*, but I was twenty-five years of age, over at Edwin's parents for Christmas, and we watched it on TV. They couldn't believe that I found it so sad, and the three of them laughed more because I was crying. I felt so misunderstood and totally humiliated. God, do I love our connections, Helen, and that core of yours makes my heart sing. Words can't really explain the sense of relief and delight I feel at our daring to write about it all. I spoke to Marnie Levitt the other day, and she said she keeps thinking of us and our letters, and how marvellous it all sounded. I think there is going to be some envy from our friends.

This is one hell of a disjointed letter, Helen. I didn't feel like writing today, but I want to post this tomorrow, so I forced myself to pick up the pen. The last couple of weeks have been scattered for me, what with the floors getting done, Amethyst having a lot of changes in staff, which is always stressful (I'll talk about that some other time) and just generally feeling stressed. I did manage to send out a number of poems to magazines and am looking into sorting out my CPP and RRSPs just in case I want to retire earlier. That is one major decision, as Amethyst has not only been my place of employment but also my community and a lot of my support, and in return it has received a lot of passion and commitment. I'll keep you posted on developments in that area.

Helen, we seem to have so much in common. Yes, I did know that you acted in a Yiddish theatre group. Maybe if things had been different for each of us, we might have acted on stage together. Another desire of mine was to be an actor professionally. I was in acting school during my early school years and, I believe, showed great promise. Mind you, that was always on my report cards—"shows great promise"! Anyway, as the money dried up—no, hardly that, as my father drank it up!—I didn't continue, but always wanted to be the world's greatest actor. No half measures, and it wasn't until Joe Dietrich from Rideauwood[14] said, "Everything that's worth doing is worth doing poorly" that things changed. I was shocked and asked him to explain, and he said that too many people are afraid of trying if they think they have to excel, so it's better to try something and enjoy what you can. Soon after that I went to Tara Players and became an amateur actor and enjoyed every bit of it. Oh the dreams "of becoming" I had! You too, Helen, you too. I hope you manage to understand my sentence structure, dear, dear friend.

>With my love and constant thoughts,
>*Oonagh xxx*

[14] Rideauwood is an addictions centre in Ottawa. I worked there before going to Amethyst.

Helen

My dear Oonagh,

Finally I am ready to write. Am spending a quiet Labour day weekend—no plans, no people, almost no phone calls, no pushing, no commitments. Thus minimal tension—there is always some tension within me as I deal with the dailyness of things, but that's a given and not troubling if it doesn't escalate. Gil is sleeping, still not completely recovered from the rotten virus that took hold this past week. There is silence in the house. Whoops, Gil just got up! A minor interruption—he's less communicative than usual when not well, which I sometimes find hard. Right now, it's fine.

I did play tennis yesterday in the gorgeous beginning fall weather—cool air, mixed sun and cloud, friendly club members who let me know I'd been missed. Hadn't played for several weeks. With my hazy, lazy weekend non-schedule, I got there late, hung around, enjoyed the tennis and the gab, left when the spirit moved me. Then I sauntered back to Botanica, sat on the bench outside, helped an elderly neighbour with her groceries (a stranger—told me she has cancer—alone and struggling) and came home refreshed, relaxed and maybe even slightly rejuvenated.

Time has been an issue for me since childhood. Probably why the timelessness of this weekend has been a joy. When I was little, we had a French-Canadian "maid" called Leontine. She was strict and probably compulsive. Yet kind. She had a thing about time and punishment. Not crime and punishment, although one could make a connection. For example, I had to be out of my bath within five or ten minutes—if not, I couldn't have peanut butter or jam for breakfast. And so on. Not tragic in the scheme of things, but a way of creating anxiety in a child re time. Both my parents were very punctual. Being late, not showing up, promising and not delivering were simply out of the question.

I like parts of this pattern, instilled it in my children, who are now much like me re time. The downside of it is the crazy-making anxiety re time that used to permeate everything I did. I've always been at airports and train stations way ahead of arrival or departure. Gil is the opposite. He can't bear the thought of wasting time (or wasting *anything*), so he mostly "just makes it."

I loved the story of your Helen insisting that you're more beautiful than her grandmother and then the two of you dissolving into hysterical laughter. What did beauty mean to you, Oonagh? It was a mixed blessing for me for a long time. It meant I was good-looking, not smart like my sister. And it meant that what I had was on the outside, not the inside. I never told my kids they were beautiful, whether they were or not, because I so wanted them to develop their inner resources and character. Undoubtedly, I carried all that to extremes. Secretly, I would get a kick out of their comments re wishing they looked more like me. As adolescents, I embarrassed the hell out of them with my grey-white hair, my pedal-pushers and my very plain clothes.

They wanted a mother who was like mothers were supposed to be—made up, dyed hair if "necessary," thin, well-dressed, not "way out" in behaviour and lifestyle (meaning proper dishes, proper furniture and proper involvements). Not a "difficult" wife. And mother, they might have added. Fortunately they didn't get what they wanted. It never occurred to me, amid their adolescent critiques, to change myself externally to satisfy their longings to fit in, via my persona.

We were at Niagara-on-the-Lake (N-O-T-L) last week, had a wonderful time together. I told the kids I thought I had been a pretty good mother. They agreed. One of those delicious moments when mostly unspoken thoughts surface and there is a kind of consensus re important stuff. Ruthie surprised us with three summer hats, in different colours, that she had brought for our threesome. One black, one purple, one rose-coloured. Made with wired brims so you can twist them into different shapes. I got the black one and wore it a lot, Ruthie the purple, which is lovely on her, Karen the rose-coloured. It's quite a tradition now, with mother and daughters to periodically buy three of the same pieces of clothing. I began it years ago when we all had blue-purple coats (remember my story[15] in *Spider Women*). Later it was three soft, cozy flannel nightgowns. And last year at N-O-T-L, three kooky cotton summer dresses. I had a bust once—bought us long, cheap dresses in Paris—sort of lounging-around-the-house things—polyester, no less, and the kids found them utterly revolting. I still have mine, wear it occasionally as kind of a housecoat when travelling.

[15] "My Cotton Blue/Mauve Coat"

About your mother and her wisdom re men. My mother used to recite "men, men, humbugging men, they're impossible nine out of ten." Not exactly poetry but a ditty reflecting women's experience with men in and out of marriage.

I was beside myself when I read about Ted Hughes and his newly released letters re himself and Sylvia Plath. In the *Globe*, Thursday, August 30, 2001. Part of the article on the second page had this heading—"Silence Added to the Tragedy of Ted Hughes." Reminded me of the article written by Geraldine Finn titled "Why Althusser Killed His Wife." The dear, old, revered Marxist philosopher had killed his wife, been declared insane and was committed to a mental hospital. His supporters and disciples, etc. all sympathized with *his* tragedy and described how argumentative and difficult said wife had been. She the provocateur, he the victim. God, Oonagh, could have been you, me, your mother, my mother, your daughter, my daughters— argumentative, difficult, refusing to conform, to accept the status quo, etc. Geraldine rewrote the original story from a feminist perspective and earned my and many others' undying gratitude for clearing some of the cobwebs out of our colonized minds.

For me, Ted Hughes is yet another example of this same syndrome. Plus the motherhood question. At the time of Sylvia's death, he had a relationship with Assia Wevill, who in 1969 killed herself and *their* daughter. From the *Globe*: "For nearly thirty years, Hughes lived with the grief of these tragedies." And "throughout this time he refused to comment on their relationship or the circumstances surrounding her death." And he concludes that her death was the result of a "pure unlucky combination of accidents." He believes that in addition to emotional and physical exhaustion,

flu and the demands of two small children, "stirrers and trouble-makers complicated our getting together again."

I haven't got words at the moment to express what I feel about Althusser and Hughes and all the other men who deem themselves the centre of the universe—individually and collectively—and wonder why a lonely single mother, a poet and perhaps a genius, who was emotionally and physically exhausted, with flu, two little kids and probably a pittance of money, would kill herself. Where in hell was the noble Ted Hughes? Why wasn't he minding the kids instead of screwing around with someone else? The question is, Why wouldn't Sylvia—or any other woman who felt entitled to a life—end it all?!? To be discussed at next lunch, I hope.

What flows from my anger at the Ted Hugheses of this world is this: that you and I have much in common, especially our passion and our rage. And we both allow for "evil thoughts." I can certainly let go in my beloved feminist groups—envisioning, books, Crones, writing. But there's something unique about a significant individual friendship that allows the complicated, and often contradictory, parts of me to surface freely. There are differences between us but there is also common ground rooted in our interests, ideas and temperaments, plus mutual curiosity re the human condition. Our friendship provides a kind of freedom I crave, like oxygen. And it's profoundly connected, for me, with being female.

What about you, Oonagh? I know this is a repetitive theme between us, but I have to ask it anyway. I can't believe that I've found a friendship in this writerly way, at this stage in my life. Thank you for having persisted with the CP idea. It has enhanced

my life immeasurably. Letters are much more than I ever imagined. Emily Dickinson knew it all along.

Wasn't bridge fun the other day? I loved winning. But as I tell Gil, who is ultra-competitive, I don't hate losing.

Lovingly,
Helen

P.S. I think I'm very old-fashioned. Been thinking a lot about the importance of character and character building. Does the subject grab you?

Oonagh

September 8, 2001

Dearest Helen,

I'm in a writing slump; all my thoughts and actions are interfering in the process of taking pen to paper. What a pain. If I weren't writing to you, Helen, I would not be writing at all. So this is probably going to be very pedestrian. I do find this humid weather extremely tiring and difficult. My mind gets fuzzy and my energy is zero. I felt so alive in the earlier part of the week. This is when I long for the moderate climate of Ireland. Summers here affect me far more than the winters. True, icy pavements bother me, and if I can't walk every day, my body seems to cease to function, and doing stretching exercises indoors doesn't do it for me in the way walking does. Well, now that I have moaned about the goddamn weather, I'll try to write about other things.

What? Well, let me see. Tara Players phoned me the other night and asked me to play the part of Cathleen Ni Houlihan in the Yeats play of that name. It is a short one-act play. Anyway, although I was glad they asked me, I said no as I find the play dull and the part of the old woman, Cathleen, uninspiring. Cathleen Ni Houlihan was the name Yeats gave to Ireland, like "My dark Rosaleen," which is

a poem written about Ireland—Mother Ireland, and her sons that die for her. Thirty years ago if I had been asked to play a part I would have jumped at it, whether I liked the part or not, but no more. After playing Kate in *Dancing at Lughnasa*, I would want a very special part before I would go on stage again. I just loved her character, and as she was so opinionated and bitchy, I didn't have to do much acting! And Brian Friel does write great plays and great parts for women. *Dancing at Lughnasa* was very autobiographical, as he grew up in a small town in County Donegal with his mother and four aunts.

Twelve noon. I have just spoken to Karin, my daughter-in-law. She is so yummy; I love her to pieces. When Niall first met her twelve years ago, he phoned me after their first date and told me he had just met the woman he was going to marry. A few weeks later, he brought her up to meet us (they were living in Toronto), and from the moment she stepped into our home, she became part of us. The first time my Helen met her, she turned to Niall and told him that if he didn't want Karin, she'd have her! Niall and she met in the workplace; she was over for a year's training from Sweden. After the year was up, she returned there and stayed for two years, trying to make up her mind whether she wanted to live in Canada. Niall, in the meantime went to live in Edmonton, and then finally B.C., as he knew that she would never come back to him if it wasn't to live beside the sea. During that two years of waiting, I suggested to him that maybe he needed to let go of Karin. His answer to me was "I am not going anywhere with anyone else, and I intend to wait her out." He did, and after two years went to Göteberg to see her and phoned me a few days later to say they were getting married. Her mother

refused to go to the wedding, and for years hardly spoke to Niall. She kept phoning Karin to come home and leave "that awful man" who smoked. This always upset Karin more than it did Niall, as he seemed to have a grudging respect for this "difficult" woman, and in the end she has accepted him. I never met her, as she refused to meet Chris and me when we went to Göteberg many years ago. Karin's father was so embarrassed and apologized. Can you imagine. Of course, having had, and still having, people saying to me how nice and kind Chris is, and how difficult I am, I could not give Karin's father any brownie points, nice guy that he is. What I loved about Karin's mother was her integrity and I do hope I meet her one day.

It's funny how history has a habit of repeating itself. Edwin's parents were so opposed to his marrying me; I was Irish, I was Catholic. They refused to come to our wedding, and not until after Niall was born did they finally come round to at least tolerating my presence in their life. One day I had a terrible fight with his mother, and she told me that I was going to give her a heart attack. Edwin and his father said I had to apologize. I refused, and a few days later, we got together by ourselves, worked it out and became friends. Many, many years later on the night that she died, I had an amazing dream, which confirmed our friendship. One day, I'll tell you about it.

Back to Karin. I believe my relationship with Karin has enhanced my relationship with Niall. They are both extremely open about their struggles together. They do seem to enjoy each other after ten years of marriage. I still think it's a good idea for a woman to marry outside her culture (that is, if she wants to get married!). No doubt it depends on the individuals, but I just think

it gives an edge to the woman, in that she can't be as easily slotted into the cultural stereotype. Yes, I know there's the whole gender stereotype that is so common to all cultures, and until we women of the world amalgamate to form our own "woman culture" regardless of man-made borders and man-made nationalism and culture, steps such as marrying outside of those cultures seem to me a tiny step for womankind. A bit muddled, is it? And totally idealistic! I use the word *colonized* to describe women's identity in the world. It was such a confirmation when you used it too, Helen. Chris goes nuts when I use it in that context. Tough shit!

Sunday, September 9

Dearest Helen, here I am again; and yet another hot steamy day. We did play tennis this morning—not for very long. I'll probably spend the rest of the day holed up in our air-conditioned home. I feel so lucky that we are able to afford it. Yet I don't consider it a luxury. I think everyone is entitled to it in these hot, humid climates. I am all set to paint a wall but not sure if I'll get down to it today. God help us when we try to sell this place. For most of my childhood and into my early teens, we lived in an old house in a small village outside Dublin. It is now a suburb, Shankill, between the mountains and the sea. As a child, I thought this house was a mansion. When I returned a few years ago, it was such a small, rundown, unattractive house. Anyway, there were many cubbyholes, and underneath the stairs was a "glory hole"; have you heard that expression? It was a small space with a door, and Brian and I used to go in there with an old gramophone and play records, and chat and giggle and make believe. It seems to me we were given a lot of time to goof off,

and to this day, Helen, daydreaming and idling are such important parts of my life. Aside from getting to school on time and doing our homework, our time was our own. That was in the early years when my father was away; everything changed when he was finally posted to Dublin.

All summer, we would be down on the beach, and while we swam and played on the rocks (it was a very stony beach), my mother would sit and knit or read. In the autumn we would walk up the mountains, picking blackberries and conkers, and in the winter evenings, I remember sitting in front of a turf fire in the cozy dining room, where my mother would read us stories and teach us all how to knit (hey, I used to be a good knitter). My father gave her very little money, but she managed to make a cozy home for us then. She had a way of decorating and arranging flowers that was very different from the usual cluttered, heavy furniture of other homes in Ireland. So, Helen, unlike your structured home life, mine was more easygoing. I think it would have been very different if my father had lived with us. When he did come home for a few days, glorious in his uniform, my mother waited on him hand and foot, and the whole household was centred on his comforts. My mother was a single mother right from the start. Most mothers were then, certainly in Ireland. She told me that my father had no time for children, and aside from me had never wanted more than one. He just about accepted Brian, so you can imagine the expectations that were placed on her by us all. She was totally responsible (and was held totally responsible) for our emotional, physical and spiritual well-being. And although Edwin was not at all like my father, as the children grew older—from infancy, that is—he was impatient

with them. So the result of that was that I, like my mother, became the person that the children turned to all the time. And of course I fucked up so many times. Some of the biggest rows we had were about his lack of support for the children. Not financially, but, for example, when I was being totally unreasonable with them, he would always side with me. Then I would turn on him for not supporting them when I was such a bitch. Crazy, eh? And then when he was unreasonable, I would support the children! Edwin was an only child, and at an early age he was told by his father to take care of his mother (his father travelled a lot), which he did, but his attitude to women was that they couldn't take care of themselves, and he believed that of me. When we separated he told a friend of mine that he didn't know how I was going to manage, and she laughed at him and said that I'd manage, all right, but she wasn't sure about him. I know, Helen, he would always have looked after me, in sickness, but for me the price was too high. I certainly would not be the woman I am today if I had stayed, as the healthier I became emotionally and spiritually, the less he could cope. I think most of the problem with Edwin was that he was, and is, a nice man, very much into the shoulds, so that he ends up doing things he doesn't really want to do.

Now, Chris is a totally different kettle of fish. From what he has told me about his past, he was very self-centred. He dearly loved his children but was too much taken up by his own writing and career to be there for them. He admits that Ulla[16] was the emotional and physical mainstay for the kids. Even though

[16] Chris's first wife

there were many things wrong and painful about my relationship with Edwin, I certainly am glad I had the children with him rather than with Chris. Even with Aaron, he (Chris) was in competition for my affection, which drove me mad. It was years before it finally sank in that there is a big difference between the love of two adults and the love of an adult for a child. It's as if he wanted to repeat his mother's love in me. Do you think most men do that, and women love men as they were loved as children, and none of us learn to love adults as adults? This is getting totally complicated, and reading over this last bit doesn't make sense to me. If you can understand it, please let me know, Helen.

I can't believe where I go with this writing, Helen. I have never written about this sort of stuff before. What a gift you have given me, allowing me in all my contradictions to ramble on and on and on. I hope I don't bore you silly. I wanted to respond to your question about beauty, but I'm tired, so will write about it another time. I look forward to our lunch on Friday.

> With my love, dearest friend,
> *Oonagh xxx*

P.S. When I was growing up, there were two postal deliveries a day, six days a week. When my mother was growing up, there were *five* deliveries a day! Can you imagine, everyone writing—no phones, and lots of work for the postmen (no postwomen in those days)!

Helen
September 16, 2001

My dear Oonagh,

I spent half the night writing to you, in my head. I'm exploding with things to say, stories to tell, feelings to share, memories to resurrect, comments and observations to register. I know what it's like to feel empty, to struggle with an internal sense of nothingness. This is the opposite: it feels like my mind or my being is too small or too narrow or too limited to cope with everything fighting for space in my head.

North America seems to have blown up this week. Tuesday, September 11, 2001. The hijacking of planes, the suicide bombers, the smashing of the Pentagon, the destruction of both towers of the World Trade Centre. More than 5,000 people dead, God knows how many injured. The brutality, the hate, the cost. I begin to grasp the meaning of the word terrorism—it is to terrorize, to instill terror in a helpless, unsuspecting civilian population. And now war is threatening from both sides of the world. We North Americans are no longer immune from civilian casualties. There is no safe place. Our world will never be the same. Never. I'm glad I am old.

I have always been terrified of physical violence, though I

have never experienced it. As a child, I covered my eyes at the movies whenever violence threatened to erupt or did. I still do. The one movie from childhood that made an everlasting impression—I think it was called *The Sign of the Cross*—had a scene with Christians being thrown into fiery ovens. I used to show Studio D films on battered women and rape to my Carleton SSW[17] students but I mostly avoided watching them. I was able to hear about violence, read about it, but seeing it with my own two eyes was like living it. I think we've all been traumatized in North America this past week, to a greater or lesser degree. And have lost confidence. Time and distance may bury September 11 in our collective unconscious, but it is likely to remain there.

I have been endlessly grateful to CBC radio for helping me to stay sane, for providing the luxury of hearing thoughtful commentators explore ways of thinking about and analyzing September 11. I've told you about the program re good and evil with Mark Kingwell and David MacGregor (sociology, University of Western Ontario). How the latter, in looking back at the history of terrorism, mentioned three major crimes against humanity—slavery, the Holocaust and the oppression of women. I literally choked up at the inclusion of women, tears came. And I realized how starved I've been, how silenced, re seriously addressing male violence against women. Men, on all sides of the struggle, are the actors and decision-makers, the ones who dominate and control governments, the military, major industries, the established institutions of each and every country and state. In the '70s, Gloria Steinem wrote a classic piece equating hatred of women with fascism. The article is

[17] Carleton University School of Social Work

probably sitting in storage with the rest of my Carleton stuff. Whoever David MacGregor is, he has my humble appreciation.

When I think of women and Afghanistan, I want the Taliban to be blasted to smithereens (knee-jerk reaction, I know). But who will be in danger, contained in their homes? The women, the small children, the girls and the sick and elderly. No answer, that. What then? What is to be done? When will men find the courage to confront one another's behaviour, to develop humility, to listen to and learn from women? For sure we're no saints, we can be cruel. But I do think partly because of mothering and motherhood (including the "mothering" of men and bosses and neighbours and friends and parents and the sick and the handicapped) that we are not interested in wars and bombs and guns and *winning* at all cost.

When you told me that your Helen had commented graphically re male violence recently and you had responded with something like "oh, yes," I felt less alone, less silenced. Then I bumped into Susan and we talked about how isolated we felt as feminists. God, if Helen and you and Susan and I are feeling isolated, what's happening to other women, everywhere? Thank God for my feminist friends and groups. But it's a far cry from our hopes and dreams and huge accomplishments of the '70s and '80s. Are we, is the contemporary women's movement again being buried—subsumed, as Adrienne Rich once wrote—by seemingly more universal crises or forms of oppression?

I was reminded yesterday of how we used to think in terms of people dying for a cause—like Buddhist monks immolating themselves as a form of protest during the Vietnam war or Emily Wilding throwing herself under a racehorse at Ascot, a martyr for the suffragette movement in England. Now it all seems to be

about slaughtering others for a cause.

Oonagh, dear friend, I can't tell you how important you are in my life. It's not just the CP; it's not just the lunches or the friendship; not the Amethyst connection, the bridge, the fun or the passion and the rage. It's—surprise, surprise—the *feminism*, as foundation. Somehow, despite disagreements some of the time, you and I know how to listen, to speak and not to judge one another as we talk. We both understand, I think, that life is inevitably bittersweet and full of contradictions, personally and politically. We seem to be able to act this out with one another, exploring rather than debating, proud of being "works in progress" (and process) rather than having illusions about knowing it all. Can't recall who said that women are curious about men, while men simply desire women.

I've had two surprising moments with good women friends yesterday and today. One was Addy, who at eighty-three is about to fly off to Japan and Bali with her daughter for a month. We spoke briefly, by phone, about the 9/11 crisis. She said that her response is to send love and energy to the world. I couldn't really respond— I'm in such a different place politically. Addy and I for years shared feminist ideas, experiences and outrage. Then Christel called and I told her about my conversation with Addy. C's response was that maybe Addy's right and perhaps it's a good way of coping. Me, I'm reminded that differences among important, old friends are inevitable and the point is to explore them.

I think I hear spoken tones *acutely*. They provide me with a lot of information, a lot of nuance, a third ear sort of. I trust my third ear. There is something about *our* connection that allows me a marvellous sense of freedom. And so, midst talking about

September 11 and other world-shaking events, I can also speak freely of the bittersweet in my life, of politically incorrect thoughts, of whom I like or don't like at the moment, for whatever cocka-mamie reasons. I absolutely loved our lunch together the other day—the talk about your Helen, of Marilyn's response to our CP, my scoop re finding socks that don't immediately slip down under the soles of my feet, your idea of using an amethyst in the women's necklace I was wearing (gift from Interval House's twenty-fifth anniversary), my lending it to you, our sheer joy at your plan. Like two kids. There's a piece in *Dropped Threads* (Carol Shields, ed.) by Isabel Huggan on how the child lives on in the aging body—extremely well done. Relevant to us.

I may hear tones in the spoken word, but I'll probably be a dud singing tones at Womansing on Wednesday night. And I'll have to stay awake and stand on my feet when I'm tired. And *work* at not ruining the sounds and the timing. I'm so pleased they hope to sing at Take Back the Night.

Life does go on. Ruthie flew to Halifax yesterday for work. Rachel leaves for India on Wednesday. And Addy goes to Japan tomorrow. Gil is at the cottage. He may be going to Prague in October with Jack, in November possibly to an Elderhostel in Hawaii (has a free ticket from agreeing to be bumped, wants to go as far as possible). Then you and Chris to Spain.

Most of my travels are internal. But soon I need to "travel" to the Carleton fitness centre. That fall down several stairs about ten days ago, face down, really shook me up. And bruised my ribs on the right side. Was painful, but has eased up considerably. Ruthie thinks I've had several lives. Somehow having Pam for massage is very reassuring. I now have a top-notch repertoire of resource

people in my life to help keep me in one piece, mentally and physically. I don't need them all the time, but they know me well and care (I think, am never 100 percent sure).

Seven pages; I wonder if you'll feel the envelope, think it's thin and be disappointed. But there's one more thing I want to say. You wrote about how your time was your own as a kid, how you could goof off. And to this day, daydreaming and "idling" (lovely old-fashioned word) remain important to you. I want to say me too, me too! No one hovered over us as kids or entertained or programmed us. My mother was an unusual Jewish wife and mother. She rode a bicycle, swam regularly at the Y, and like you, Oonagh, walked everywhere. In those days, Jewish girls in Ottawa mostly didn't have bikes, weren't allowed to do overnight canoeing as my sister and I were, lived more indoors than outdoors. We were all being groomed for men and marriage. It was my mother who encouraged and allowed our adventures. She started the first Jewish Girl Guide troop in Ottawa. I loved Guide camp in particular—a primitive, $5-a-week, living-in-tents and sleeping-on-straw-palliasses kind of camp—classless and sporty. And it's where I first began to love singing—lustily!

Enuf! This is the end. Sun and blue sky beckon, and I've been sitting on my ass for far too long. See you at Womansing.

Lots of love,
Helen

P.S. Just found your poem "Cattigollager" in one of your envelopes. Imagine, writing a love poem to a small mountain! Creative Oonagh, literal Helen.

Oonagh

Saturday, September 22, 2001,
7:30 p.m., in the kitchen

Dearest friend,

The rain is pouring down. I just love the sound of it; and Chris has gone to listen to Bernard MacLaverty, an Irish writer, who is speaking at the National Arts Centre. I rarely go to readings these days. I used to go to all of them, but I've lost interest unless it's someone very special. Maybe if they were in the morning I'd go, but I am very tired by evening and want to just veg out, or play Upwords or watch TV. I have wondered about this, but I think it's because I give 100 percent of my energy—spiritually, emotionally and physically—to everything I do during the day, be it my work, lunching with friends, singing, writing or just goofing off, that I wear out by seven! Does that make sense? I do love my passion, but it's certainly hard to live with! Helen, your loving, bitchy letter was a tonic.

A number of years ago, Chris and I were over at our friends Vicki and Tony's for dinner with some of their friends, and Tony reacted to something I said about the lack of power women had. After about ten minutes of back and forth, I finally told him to phone up a professor in women's studies, read some material on

the history of women and then maybe I would consider discussing the issue with him. I remember the stunned silence when I said it. I don't think Tony ever took me up on my suggestion, but Vicki has quoted me often. She thinks that was one of the best comments she had ever heard at a dinner party. Mouthy, eh? It amazes me that I have any friends left, not you or Marilyn[18], but female friends who buy the (male) party line, for the most part anyway. I buy into it too at times, but maybe the difference is that I know I'm doing it, and for whatever reason, be it tiredness or that I just can't be bothered arguing, I let things go.

I woke up this a.m. very down again; I feel my whole being is in shock most of the time after what has just happened. I push myself to go out for a walk. I read the odd newspaper such as the *Guardian Weekly* and odd bits of info that my Helen sends me by e-mail, and Chris, who looks very sad most of the time, and I talk about our horror and our fears, and we also try and escape from it; like last night when we went to the movies—*Green Fingers* with Helen Mirren. It was funny and gentle and just what we both needed. My son Niall phoned today and said that he would find it very strange if I wasn't reacting to this catastrophic disaster in the way I am. I was very comforted by his thoughtful words. And then I had a phone call from my sister, and that was great too.

My brother Brian, was in Egypt on September 11, so when he got home, Eithne phoned to find out how he was and what the reaction in Egypt was; and he told her that he didn't want to talk about it. I tried to send him an e-mail last week when I heard where he was, but it didn't get delivered. I think I will always

[18] Marilyn Benoit, longtime close friend

have a little hope that one day he will write to me and say, "I love you, Oonagh."

Helen, do you think there might be a possibility that they, the U.S. and their cohorts, could possibly blow the Taliban regime to smithereens without killing any women and children? On the BBC News tonight, I heard that the commentators think they can. I doubt it. It's a great disappointment to me that the U.S. has turned out the way it has, as, when I was growing up, Boston was a mecca for the Irish people, more so than Rome, at least for us atheists and half-baked Catholics. It wasn't until I joined the peace movement that I began to see them in a different light—not the individuals, but their foreign and domestic policies. Domestic in that you have to have pots of money to get into the White House, and probably three-quarters of U.S. citizens don't vote. As for their foreign policy, I don't trust them an inch. Friends today are gone tomorrow. And although I am shocked at Israel's continuing to build settlements, at this moment in time I fear that the U.S. is going to turn against them completely. I must be very politically naïve, Helen, as I was not fully aware that the critics of U.S. policy abroad blamed the continued U.S. support of Israel as one of the main reasons why this all happened. I know little or nothing about the Balfour Declaration of 1917, but, coming from Ireland, I am extremely suspicious of anything the British Empire had anything to do with. I question their motives, as I question those of the U.S. today. For years I put Israel on a pedestal. I had read much about the political and cultural dreams of the early Zionists. One of my heroes was Ben-Gurion, alongside Michael Collins! So, my dear Helen, I can't stand it when the Israeli government does something (or doesn't do something) and opens itself to be criticized by both

enemies and friends alike. And then I have to go full circle and acknowledge that, as in every other country in the world, the splitting of lands by borders will always cause wars in our patriarchal societies. Aside from token women who pay lip service to the status quo, women are not part of it, except to pick up the pieces and become the spoils of war. I sometimes sit in a corner of a room and howl in rage and powerlessness. Very sane image, eh? So dearest, dearest Helen, I hope what I have said doesn't offend you, and if it does I hope you will tell me. I have no doubt whatsoever that our magical way of listening to each other will carry us through our differences. It's truly amazing that I have managed to write at all. I can so relate to Aharon Appelfeld when he said a few days ago how difficult it was to write: "It is hard to be with oneself when everything around is burning." I have many of his books; I love the simplicity of his writing.

Sunday, September 23

I have just watched the *Life and Times* documentary on Pierre Elliott Trudeau. I would love to have met him. I told Chris that once, and he wrote to Hugh MacLennan[19] (who was a friend of Trudeau's) and asked him if he could arrange a lunch for Trudeau and me. Needless to say it never happened, as MacLennan himself had not seen him for years. Chris didn't let me know he had done that until after the fact. Mind you, I didn't like everything he did. I wanted to leave Canada during the War Measures crisis. The younger brother of one of my colleagues got fifteen months in jail because he was on the

[19] the well-known Canadian novelist

fringes of the separatist movement; he was seventeen years of age. Disgusting!

Tuesday, September 25

What a bloody messy letter; put it down to the times we live in! I continue to feel so anxious about the world situation and about Amethyst—I miss Jane's aura, and we have six new staff and there is a crazy bustle about the place, which is anything but restful. And, then, there's my son Paul, and his wife Terri, and newborn daughter Rachel. Terri is very depressed. They have hardly any money, and Paul is finding it extremely difficult to go to work and leave Terri and Rachel. They have isolated themselves, so have very little support.

I have to go to work shortly. I do feel a little vulnerable about this letter, so no doubt I will phone you in a few days to get reassurance that you and I can climb the mountains and dip into the valleys of our friendship and survive—hey, poetic, don't you think!

With my love,
Oonagh xxx

Oonagh

Dearest Helen,

Once more I'm in the kitchen, on my own, as Chris has gone to have dinner with Christel and Manfred. I declined, as they are having sausages and (ugh) sauerkraut. Christel was very concerned that I would feel left out. No way. I am so delighted to have the house to myself. In particular, to be able to write to you, and from the kitchen. Today, I feel I am finally over my despair and horror at the happenings in the world. Not that anything is resolved; on the contrary, but I feel I'm finally back inside myself. (Does that make sense to you?) And can once more try to make a difference to my own life and maybe, by chance, to those whom I love and cherish. I hope that doesn't sound Pollyannaish.

I have had a very peaceful day, just pottering about. Talked to my sister and told her that her voice seems so much lighter these days, and she said she believes it's because she's dumped the antidepressants. Nothing like getting angry, taking action and feeling in control! I am delighted with the changes, but I am also a little wary. We have never spoken to each other like this before. Today, she was quick to ask how I was and how I was

90

managing to cope with the way I was feeling these last weeks. I could hardly tell her, as I was so surprised at her question. Helen, it was strange, but so nice. We did talk a little at how delighted we both are with this burgeoning friendship (maybe, maybe, maybe!).

Last night, I went to Donna and Jane's "leaving" party. For the most part, it was marvellous—laughter, tears, good, good memories—and I sang, Helen, on my own, two songs. Can you imagine? The first one I sang was "They Can't Take That Away from Me" to Donna. We stood together, holding hands, looking into each other's eyes—truly a love song. I had thought I was going to ham it up, but when I stood looking at her, what came out of my mouth was the opposite. Everyone in the room was crying. It was an amazing moment for us all, and then I sang "Every Time We Say Goodbye" to both Jane and Donna. Today, I can't believe I dared, but there you are, I did, and Donna said she was thrilled to pieces. I sent an e-mail to my singing teacher and told her that I did it, and she was pleased and said she was very proud of me. God, Helen, I sound like a little girl, don't I? Well, my mother always said that her heart stopped getting old at eighteen, so even in her old body she still felt like a young woman.

Tuesday, October 2, 2001

I love when I wake up in good humour. I did this morning, having had a lousy day at work yesterday; it was totally chaotic. Carol came in, didn't say good morning to anyone, just informed staff what she wanted us to do. I stayed in my office with the door closed all day, except for running a group. Her redeeming

words to me were "You have a lovely singing voice, and maybe we could use you to do a benefit for us!" I wish she hadn't said that, as I don't want to be distracted from my evil thoughts about her! Today, I'm going in for only four hours and tomorrow is my last day until November 5. I have filled out my Canadian Pension Plan forms, all ready to go if things get to the point that I can't cope with it anymore. We have six new staff, and in an agency of thirteen that is very stressful. I'll stop here, or my bad humour will return. I have also decided not to look at news on TV any-more—the whole CBC bombardment on the subject of September 11 and what the U.S. is doing and not doing; and poor old Chrétien (I never thought I would say anything good about him) constantly being criticized for lack of security, etc.; and hardly anything at all about the individual people who were blown to pieces, their lives over and their families' lives in shatters. I just hate it all, and as I have no input into anything they decide to do, it's better for me to return to the local—sing, write letters to you, play tennis or Upwords, read and go to see the women at work. And on Thursday we are playing bridge. I would love to play it more often.

Wednesday, October 10

Well lovey, what a disjointed letter this is. Yesterday was taken up by "going or not going" on our trip to Spain and Ireland. We are going and it's only me that goes up and down. Chris just stands there and waits until I make up my mind, which drives me crazy, and yet I admire his ability not to get into my turmoil. Although his silence drives me nuts 'cause I then have to listen to myself and work out my own fears without his input.

We are very different in that way, as I almost always like to have other opinions about my decisions, and when I voice something to someone, Chris or a friend, it's because I haven't made up my mind. Whereas Chris thinks it all out in his own head first and then presents it, a *fait accompli*.

Many years ago when we went to a marriage counsellor, I complained that he never responded to my opinions and that I was left feeling unheard, not listened to, and sensed a total lack of interest on his part. His response was that I always came across as so sure of myself and he felt that I was never wanting his opinion around certain issues. It was such an eye-opener for me. We were, and continue to be, so different in the way we communicate. Chris still works things out in his own head and then tells me about his decision. Because of my uproar, he is somewhat more attentive to my need to discuss. This is not what I intended to write about today, but what the hell.

Helen, the half -hour we spent on Sunday evening was like a little oasis. I felt very close to you. My angst about relationships, work, war, etc., can never compare to my total agony and anxiety around Helen and Aaron. You talk about your third eye, Helen, well I too experience a third eye; however, with Aaron and Helen, I don't even have to see them. I just know when things are not okay with one or other of them. I also feel it with Paul and Niall, but not as much, maybe because they live some distance away, and also their lives have not been as up and down as Helen's has. I have tried over the years to protect myself, but I don't find that easy to do. Still, I am getting better. I don't ask too many questions anymore, and when they don't phone, I assume everything is all right, and I don't go looking. So, dearest Helen,

what a very mixed blessing this mothering/grandmothering is. I rage about it a lot.

During the last few years of her life, my mother told me over and over again that she wished she had not had children. I'm glad she didn't tell me that when I was younger as I would certainly have felt she didn't love me. But our relationship turned into a grand friendship in her later years, so that it was not an emotional issue but an issue to be talked about by two women (mother/daughter/friends!).

Dearest Helen, please take great care of yourself while I'm away. Whatever I experience will be with you in mind.

<div align="right">

With my love,
Oonagh xxx

</div>

$$\mathcal{H}elen$$

October 6, 2001

My dear Oonagh,

I've been full of *mea culpas* this week because I haven't met my own deadline for writing to you. By my calculations, I am several days late. However, I have many worthy rationalizations—like long Thanksgiving weekend will be quiet and conducive to writing; like my aging body can only handle so much pressure and busyness (I use this one a lot when push comes to shove); like I have to buy sturdy new pads of paper before I can write, as the skinny half-used ones aren't supportive enough if I sit in the living room chair, pad on crossed knees. And I have to test out how Oonagh will react if I screw up etc., etc. I can share all this garbage with you because the *mea culpas* are half serious and half in fun.

There's a lot to tell you about. Especially what happened to me yesterday morning in the Carleton fitness centre where I do my thrice-weekly mix of stretching/yoga/exercises, all on a mat for at least an hour and a half. Have you ever been there? The place is full of exercise machines, almost unbearable noise called music by contemporary youth, many men and some women, and

a half dozen thick gym mats, one of which is longer than the rest. I dive for the long mat—more space for my body, and it's located next to a piece of apparatus that helps to get me up and down. Sort of a bar to grab hold of. If this mat isn't free, I position myself close to it, on one of the smaller mats, keeping an eagle eye out to see when someone vacates my chosen spot, at which point I wiggle my ass over to grab it. You get the picture?

This is the last place in the world you would ever expect me or anyone else to be introspective, daydreamy, imaginative. But strangely enough, I, who require solitude and silence and aloneness in my life, lie on the mat and somehow enter into a cocoon where I roam around internally in rich and surprising ways.

What happened yesterday was that I felt *writerly*. My head was just spinning, deliciously, with all kinds of ideas, experiences, moments and memories. Totally unexpected, just a burst of spontaneity in all directions. I was writing to you in my head and trying to hold on to all the fragments that kept surfacing. Most important was a memory of being on a plane, writing furiously as though my life depended on it, on a pad of foolscap like this one, about feminist counselling. The ideas kept coming more rapidly than I could write them down. I would lose them and find them and then hatch more. Sort of like the multiplying brooms in *Fantasia*.[20] Observing my intensity, a flight attendant asked me what I was working on. It was my first experience—other than journals or diaries—of catching a glimpse of what "real" writers mean when they describe the compulsion to write, the craving, the

[20] the early Disney animated film

obsession, the drivenness. And here it was happening in, of all places, the fitness centre. I can't really recapture the content or even all of the emotions. But it felt as if I was finally understanding what it means to write; that everything in one's life is grist for the mill, positively or negatively, as much trivia as world-shaking events; all of it matters and is an ingredient of individual or collective significance. I'm struggling to find words; it's not nearly as fluent right now as it was in my head at the gym.

I guess I've always known the above, intellectually. But yesterday was new. It was as though the "knowledge" dancing around in my head was at the same time seeping into my very bones and I was truly rejoicing. On that mat, in that crazy fitness centre, with all the noise, the machines, the men....

Feeling writerly was a gift. It is less than being a writer but more than being whoever I was before. Thanks for listening to my muddled, cockamamie descriptions of life in the gym, on the mat, in the head of your devoted friend and correspondent. How in hell did you and I manage to survive before we inaugurated our precious CP?

This is Sunday morning. Went to see *When Brendan Meets Trudy* last night at the Bytown with Ruthie and Larry. Ruthie and I loved it. I realize how hungry I am for wild, adventurous, spontaneous ingredients in my life. The movie figuratively fed me some of that food for the spirit. I know you and Chris were at the film—the kids saw you. Did you like it? Wish you had been sitting beside me, to translate/repeat lots of the Irish lines I missed.

The best thing you and I ever did in structuring our CP was deciding there were no expectations of responses to each other's

writing other than the next letter. It works beautifully for me, has given me a delicious sense of freedom. But I want to respond to your dinner party story and to your evolving relationship with Eithne. God, why do Irish names have to have such complicated spelling—like Niall (I always thought of him as Neil).

I loved what you told the guy at the party re getting educated, learning about women from those in the know. We feminists tended to waste a lot of time and energy explaining things to men who never bothered to do their homework. There was a veritable renaissance of knowledge in almost every sphere of life between the late 1960s and the early 1990s. There was so much to be learned, personally and politically, from the explosion of contemporary feminism and the truly remarkable achievements of the autonomous women's liberation movement. A great deal was accomplished by women with few resources except for themselves, other women and the power of ideas and the search for justice. The world today could be very different if the momentum that gave birth to the women's movement had been appreciated, nurtured, developed and sustained.

Instead, of course, we were laughed at, sabotaged, undermined and often destroyed. We were permitted to survive as long as "they," in their benevolence, chose to allow us to exist. The institutional and the material resources were never ours to control. At the university and at home, the men often made minor accommodations, but mostly they didn't think of themselves as illiterate if they hadn't studied the redefinitions of the world that feminism was all about. Seriously, in depth, with the curiosity and the dedication that they bring to science, to technology, to war.

I used to be flattered when men bothered to raise feminist issues with me. No longer, though I still engage occasionally. Mostly I want to talk with women. It's painful to think that the inspiring ideal of feminism now gets referred to as the F-word, if referred to at all.

I'm jealous of your blossoming connection with Eithne. And I think it's a lovely development for both of you. There is something about kin. I haven't given up on my sister; it's a thin connection. I used to think social workers who deemed communication central in their assessments of clients' problems were misguided. I give more weight now to personal and interpersonal communication, but only when connected to context, i.e., power versus powerlessness. And to acknowledgment of personal vulnerability, fears and painful experience. God, Oonagh, these subjects are all too big and overwhelming. I feel less and less articulate, more and more exhausted. Where's my little cocoon at the gym!

I think I've told you how Donna called me last Sunday about the conference on "Women's Resistance, from Victimization to Criminalization," sponsored by the Elizabeth Fry Society and the Canadian Association of Sexual Assault Centres. Three days—I knew I couldn't handle that physically. Donna, with her vitality and drive and remarkable commitment to women, offered to pick me up at 8 a.m., found out how I could get in for just the morning plenary, reminded me Sally was on the program (ex-student, friend), etc., etc. So I went and heard Landon Pearson, M.P. Hedy Fry (better than usual) and Sunera Thobani[21].

[21] former president of the National Action Committee on the Status of Women

Most of the audience of five hundred applauded Sunera several times throughout her speech and gave her a standing ovation. Sally too. Not me—I was stunned.

Donna was sympathetic to Sunera's relentless diatribe (my word) re American imperialism, found much of what she said to be true, was confused by my response. I also agreed with some of the content but was disturbed by her lack of compassion for the September 11 events in New York. There was something in her "tone" (remember my third ear) that felt absolute, reminiscent of every fundamentalist of every religion and every political movement within my memory.

So Donna and I talked. I said Sunera reminded me of my own absolutism when I had a single-minded Marxist analysis of capitalists and capitalism and liberal democracy and God knows who and what else. Knowing and understanding very little, closed to new ideas and possibilities, led by men, disconnected in any political sense from most women. I have few regrets about my political adventures in those days—it was an attempt to understand myself and the world. But I was blinded to many realities, always finding excuses for anything the Soviet Union did (including exploitation of women, anti-Semitism and widespread killings). I also said to Donna that the whole question of gender, the oppression of women worldwide gets lost amid this kind of politics and world-view. I'm very mixed up re how to think, what I feel, but I do know that uninterrupted absolutism and hatred won't help.

Oonagh, from way down deep I want to thank you for what you said at bridge about the thin line between the harsh critique of Israel and underlying anti-Semitism. I have a lump in my

throat and tears threatening as I write this. It was terribly important for me to hear that. More on this some other time.

Donna dropped in to Botanica the day after we heard Sunera, to further clarify the issues. She is such a delight, forever searching, forever stimulating, going beyond where most of us are at. She and my daughter Karen have made a connection. Donna now uses the beta-blockers Karen discovered to control her panic about public speaking. We're all in the midst of trying to get tickets to the gala dinner for Doris Anderson's eightieth birthday to be celebrated on November 9. The tickets have gone like hotcakes. I gave a contribution to Doris Anderson's Women's Studies Scholarship Fund ages ago but forgot to order tickets. Why am I so bloody impractical! Now Karen has to try to pick up the pieces for all of us.

This is it, Oonagh. I'm tuckered out, another old-fashioned expression. Want to grab something to eat before I listen to Susan Sontag on *Writers and Company* re love and war in relation to September 11.

Have a wonderful trip to Spain and Ireland. Fly safely, dear friend. I'll miss you, but I'll also know you're connecting with me via our CP process as I will be with you. I absolutely love our invention, Oonagh. It feels as if we've made the discovery of the century.

Lots and lots of love,
Helen

P.S. Please make me a copy of this letter when you return and send back enclosed song sheet. Would you consider joining me in a two-woman singing act, with a repertoire of all the old schmaltzy songs, which we would act out in various dramatic ways? As you did with your Donna at her farewell party? Clearly, given my limited stamina, I am going mad! Again!

Luv,
me

Oonagh

Saturday, October 20, 2001,
Mallorca, in the city of Palma

Dearest Helen,

At last. I have wandered around looking for a space to write to you and finally this is it. I complained so much about the smell in the other room that to shut me up they gave us this bright, airy room overlooking the rooftops. Chris has gone to look at some more stonework in the shape of castles and churches; you'd think he was a Catholic! I just want to sit and look at the sea, watch the people and generally potter about. This is our third visit to Palma/Mallorca in eight years, so I am beginning to feel at home. It's truly a lovely island, and I probably would never have come if brother Niall didn't live here.

Yesterday we went across the island on a train, into the mountains. It was stunning: olive groves, orange and lemon trees everywhere and blooming morning glories in every crevice. I regret not taking my hiking shoes (which you bought me for my sixtieth birthday!). I don't think I paid much attention to the planning of this trip. Barcelona is a lovely city, but three days would have been plenty for me. Instead we were there for six days. The result is that Chris and I have had

our moments and hours of hating each other's guts, he thinking I am always complaining, and me thinking he's an insensitive jerk. Today we like each other, mainly because I got my own way about changing the fucking room. Mind you, before he left, he said he would remind me of my delight at the room when I was up at 2 a.m. and bitching at him for moving about in the bed. The other room had twin beds; this one has just a double!

I think I like the idea of holidays and travel more than the actual doing, unless we stay in the same place for a length of time. I could see us in the future renting a place here, and Chris going off to other places on his own, although he doesn't seem to want to do that as much now.

We are seeing a lot of my brother and his extended family. He is extremely generous and obviously delighted to see me, telling us again and again how grateful he is that we took the time to come and see him. He is rather isolated here, as he doesn't speak Spanish, so the only one he talks to on a regular basis is Judy, his wife. The first night we were here we spent with him on his own, as Judy was in England, and he cooked us a wonderful meal. He still has a lot of anger around the neglect and abuse he suffered in childhood and why wouldn't he? I have a lot of compassion for him, as he is severely dyslexic and has had enormous barriers to overcome both socially and in his work situation. He is an amazing chef—self-taught, but nowadays most of the chefs have diplomas, etc., and look down on Niall as lesser than. Last year, the union and management tried to get rid of him, but the head boss told them they could all leave, but Niall was staying; that was such a boost to his ego.

Sunday, October 21

Another one of my disjointed letters. I seem to give you lots of fragments of news and thoughts, skipping all over the family history. Last night we went out to dinner with Judy's mother, Jeanne, and her new husband, Desmond. Aside from the fact that we ate at 10 p.m.—mussels, escargots, amazing fish that I had never heard of—we had a lovely evening. This morning, though, my gut is not too great, so a day of starvation is in sight for me. By the way, we both slept well in the double bed!

Judy's mother is just terrific; eighty-two years of age; decided a few years ago to sell her house in Norfolk, England and come over here with Desmond. They had a whirlwind romance. Both their spouses had died a few years earlier, and they met while walking their dogs; discovered they both loved dancing, so off they went into the sunset, hand in hand. They seem to enjoy each other's company and have bought and renovated an old house here that we are going to see today. The amazing coincidence is that Desmond grew up in the same place where Niall was born and where we all lived for a number of years before moving to Shankill. Desmond's father was my mother's dentist. So here are these two women, mother and daughter, English to the core, ending up with two Irishmen from the same area of Dublin.

As I write that, I think of Edwin and Chris, who were both born in London within the sound of Bow Bells, which makes them Cockneys. Did you ever see the movie *Six Degrees of Separation*? And another even weirder coincidence is that Niall and Judy lived in a place called Gee Cross near Manchester, a tiny little village. They lived in a row house, and Edwin's grandfather had lived in the house next door.

Anyway, enough of all this. Getting back to Jeanne—Judy's father died when she was about eight, and Jeanne was a single mother with two children. She went to teachers' college and became a teacher, then met her second husband, Donald, whom we met many years ago. They both loved sailing, and Jeanne is a very fine watercolour painter, so that when the two children left, they sailed all over the seas, and Jeanne painted. Desmond is also a painter, taught fine arts in a school in England.

> *Tuesday, October 23*
> *in a town square, Sitges*

What a very messy letter this is, dearest Helen. Each day I have promised myself I'd finish it, and each day goes by and I don't. This time I am definitely going to. This has not been a very restful holiday so far, but yesterday we found this lovely little town just south of Barcelona and will stay until tomorrow, when I fly to Dublin and Chris potters about for three days along the coastline north of Barcelona. We meet up in Heathrow on Sunday to return. Already one of the planes we were to take back yesterday from Mallorca to Barcelona has been cancelled. So I hope the rest of them (I still have to take four more) will be okay.

I think I was telling you about Jeanne. Well, on Saturday Niall and Judy spent the day with us driving around bits of the island, and then we went to have tea with Jeanne and Desmond. I literally wept when I saw their home. It is so beautiful, in a small village close to Palma—three patios, tiled and wood floors, paintings, books, furniture they'd had in England and looked as if it was made for the place. They finally moved in last November and it's as if they had lived there for centuries. Neither of them

speaks Spanish. No one in the village speaks English, but some-how they manage. I asked Jeanne did she miss her friends, as she had lived most of her life in Norfolk, and she said she doesn't as many of them are dead, and those that she does see come and visit for weeks. One of her old friends was with them when we visited. Still, I must say I admire their courage and tenacity although I'm still not sure why Jeanne married again; Desmond did sweep her off her feet in a way. If Chris died, I just can't see myself living with another man, but who knows what I'd do if I was in that situation? My God, Helen, we are definitely going to have to edit these letters carefully before they can be published or we won't have anyone talking to us! Mind you, we can always change their names and locations, and deny it was them. We can write a disclaimer in the front, saying it is coincidence only!

I think of you and chat with you in my head and imagine your voice and your laugh, and continue to delight in what we are doing together.

I'm going to finish this and post it now. Not as long as usual, but at least it's something. So, dearest Helen, I will accept no excuses when you take off for San Miguel. Letters continue no matter where we are.

> With my love, dear friend
> *Oonagh* xxx

Helen
October 21, 2001

My dear Oonagh,

What you and I have in common is the need, the ongoing need, to have space to ourselves—houses or condos or rooms of one's own. The theme keeps reappearing in our letters. Gil is at the cottage again this weekend, and when I awakened this morning it was with such a feeling of peace and tranquility. Of me being content in my aloneness and space and of Gil being content in his aloneness and space and of the two of us being more in sync in our old age than we ever were in our younger years. I think I felt pulled and pushed to do and be so many things when I was younger that I seldom ever could quietly be me, whoever that was. And aloneness seemed to equate with failure of various kinds—no friends, no interests, no life, no community.

My vivid memories of those trade union dances Gil and I went to in the '50s and '60s during his CUPE [22] years stand out. I loved to dance. I needed diversion, I wanted to be part of Gil's world in the labour movement, and at a distance I revered trade unionists

[22] Canadian Union of Public Employees

and activists. I always longed for connections. Grrrr! The "dances" were orgies of drinking, nauseating sexist behaviour and jokes that either silenced women or produced phony laughter in those of us who were trying desperately to fit in. I had a smile plastered all over my face until it hurt. And I remember feeling more and more inadequate because I was a wet blanket who didn't know how to have fun. Why on earth do I remember that Gil's boss used to repeatedly refer to his wife's breasts as grapefruits and then holler with laughter. There was no music, only rock and roll noise. There was no conversation worthy of the name. There was no intimacy with the guy who took you to the dance. Gil and the other men were too busy impressing their "brothers," jacking up their own egos. The women were there as window dressing. By the time we got home from these august occasions, I was seething with accumulated grievances and insults and vowing never to go again. But I did.

It took me a long time to learn what I needed and wanted, to find the courage to live it. Looking back on that terrible depression I had four years ago, when I couldn't be alone, couldn't sleep, couldn't connect, responded to nothing and no one—I think that was a turning point. Somehow I found and liked the centre of me in a newer and richer way after living through that hell. I had written in the past about how, with depression, the "plant" has to shut down when working and living conditions are unhealthy. Until now, I hadn't put pen to paper about this last experience.

Letters—to you—with our CP are oh, so surprising. I have millions of other things to tell you about, but the unexpected always slips out. The learnings from my last depression have to do with aloneness and separateness and a peaceful centre. Not to

imply that things don't go haywire and I can't lose my cool or have "evil thoughts." Or that the passion and intensity are no longer part of me. It's that there's a sturdier centre at the core of me. Hallelujah!

Faith, Jane and I saw *A Room of One's Own* at the Arts Centre, with Kelli Fox, directed by Micheline Chevrier. It was a gem! I had seen it done last year at the Shaw Festival, appreciated it then. But this time was a rare experience, and we revelled in the performance, the words of Virginia Woolf, the direction, the movement, the connectedness to our own lives. It was a moment in time when I truly grasped the significance of theatre at its very best. One of the regrets in my life is not having pursued amateur theatre more aggressively and imaginatively. I was always envious of women in Winnipeg who could be part of the Nellie McClung Theatre group. Or was it called the Redlight Theatre??

Want to form a theatre group for older women with me, Oonagh? Along with our song and dance routine? Seriously, I'm probably not going to continue with Womansing. Now that it's dark by 6 p.m., and rainy and cold, I'm shaky about going out by myself in the evening. Last Wednesday, after fully intending to go, I decided at the last minute to stay home. I'll go one more evening to return the tapes and say goodbye. Of lesser importance, but present, are my feeling of not knowing the women in the group, the absence of check-ins as a way of getting to know them, and my wanting to sing but not wanting it to be hard work. Hope my dilettante ways don't disappoint you.

Your birthday gift, which I opened on October 15, was just "write." Intriguing slip of the pen. There was the booklet about Virginia Woolf and the photographer whom I had never heard of

and the two exquisite photographs. Plus the stamp, re letters, which you drew my attention to. Everything seemed to come together and I am everlastingly impressed with your imagination. Thank you, dear Oonagh, thank you.

My seventy-eighth birthday was lovely. Cards, flowers, phone calls, gifts. I love being remembered, being the centre of attention, being loved. From your last letter "God, Helen, I sound like a little girl, don't I" (re singing teacher's comments). The truth is we remain little girls all our lives, and I think that's A-okay.

Ruthie bought me a fleecy red vest to keep my chest warm on wintry days. It feels just right and will become part of my "uniform," a piece of clothing that just fits me and my personality and my comfort zone. I get addicted to clothes and go on binges of wearing things out continuously.

Karen and I and two of her feminist friends in Toronto are going to Doris Anderson's gala eightieth birthday celebration at the Royal York in Toronto. I am thrilled. I don't know Doris but I've always been impressed with her kind of feminist leadership—from *Chatelaine*, to the National Advisory Council on the Status of Women, her famous resignation from the council around the constitutional conference in 1982 (the Axe Axworthy period[23]) and her autobiography where she claims her "illegitimate" birth.

I miss you, Oonagh, but am not worried that you won't return safe and sound. I couldn't bear not having you in my life. I'm rethinking friends these days, realizing that there are stages

[23] when Lloyd Axworthy, the federal minister, had argued against including an equal status of women section in the constitution and cancelled a women's conference on the constitution

in friendship, as there are with partners and kids. Different needs at different times, for different reasons. True friendship, to me, was always an absolute, an enduring love. But I'm not so sure. Is this the "little girl" in me?

Ruthie came over at noon to take me shopping—one of my birthday requests. In short order, I had desperately needed winter boots, underwear, long-sleeved cotton tops, leggings (for yoga) and a sort of ballet-type slipper with a rubber base so I won't break my neck on the indoor stairs. Unheard of accomplishments for me—am a lousy shopper who gives up very quickly and often gets nothing done. I actually like the parent-child reversal in this area, me the helpless puppy following along, Ruthie the take-charge adult.

Monday morning, I'm not feeling well. Have been constipated for longer than usual, resorted to cooked prunes and flaxseed, now have abdominal discomfort. Unusual. Should go to my GP. Hate the thought of having tests or getting involved in medical stuff. Little trust, or confidence in the medical model. Will go to Carleton gym later this morning despite malaise; have to keep my legs working as much as possible. Have visions of a prolonged illness when I won't be able to exercise and my legs will stiffen permanently.

God, this is a ghastly ending to this letter. I hate illness. Often say that I've finally learned how to survive and thrive and want to enjoy the harvest for a while before I croak. I love that word *croak*, it's so expressive. Does the sound of croaking have a special appeal? Or is it simply a euphemism for dying, ending, suffering?

After all the above and a few phone calls, I'm feeling much

better. Still waffling about seeing my GP, thinking it was likely a false alarm.

Change of mood, how typical of me. Am sitting in my favourite spot in the living room. In the green chair, by the bay windows with the warm sun streaming in upon me. The tall trees with their golden, green, brown leaves in the stillness of the day, the sun shining through the foliage. I am especially appreciative of joys and pleasures that are soon to end. Like October with autumn leaves and hot sun and open windows and a final few tennis games outdoors. Which is why I'm more appreciative of my life at this point in time.

Oonagh, my dear, can you bear all this stuff about my feeling ill, about endings and mortality and croaking? I hope so, because at my new and august age of seventy-eight, it's part of my reality.

I have a friend who has worked very hard all her life (now in her sixties) against all kinds of odds, has achieved much, lived through separation-divorce, alienated kids and a few years of addiction. Despite a new and well-earned equilibrium and good feelings about her own growth and development, she is angry. A part of the rage—there are many parts—is that from childhood on, things have always been serious, earnest, demanding. No fun, no laughter, no room for her gypsy-like temperament. She became a caretaker of the family in her early teens. Some parallels with you re caretaking and emigrating and a postponed adolescence. But unlike you, she hasn't taken hers yet. Fascinating connection between anger, premature responsibility (all women, but some more than others) and the human need to play, to have fun, to be wild.

Welcome home, Oonagh. You will have this in the mail when you return. I will rest easier to know you are within reach. And I can't wait to hear about all your adventures, internal and external. You have become an important part of my life.

With much love,
Helen

Helen

October 24, 2001

My dear Oonagh,

What kind of magic is this that our CP has created? Your voice on the phone, from a little town outside Barcelona, Spain, letting me know you've just "posted" (I use *mail*, you use *post*) your letter within the two-week arrangement. And that you're still writing. You gladden my heart, Oonagh Berry, with your delicious, impish, wild surprises. I loved hearing your voice from all the way across the ocean and from Spain, a country I've always wanted to visit. To answer my own rhetorical question, yes, yes, yes, there *is* magic in our CP and it seems to bring out the best in me, the very best. In you too?

There are many parts to the joy that emanates from our CP. The one that's front and centre is how childlike we both are in our excitement, our bursting-with-joy kind of intensity, our zany pleasure in sharing on paper any and all things. I want to start a worldwide movement among women to transform the planet. It has to do with pen pals—not the proper kind from my youth, but a new variety rooted in breaking the silence, consciousness-raising and the liberation of girls and women. In other words, we'll have

women all over the world participating in CPs. We'll somehow have to forge a coalition with Ruthie's literacy movement to make it global and maybe with CBC Radio to get the word out. Ruthie and Karen would be great assets. And your Helen would have to be with us on the steering committee to contribute her guts and her human-rights-are-women's-rights approach (whoops, it's the other way round, isn't it—women's rights are human rights).

I think you're going to have to retire! If we're going to be a golden oldies singing duo and we're going to pioneer a theatre group for older women and we're going to save the planet with women pen pals, it'll be a bit time-consuming. How will we find time to continue our own CP? Besides, it's quite clear that retirement is not necessarily a quiet time in life. If you're wondering about my sanity at this point, carry on. I'm into my megalomaniac phase, when hopes and dreams and fantasies rush around in my head like the brooms in *Fantasia*.

This morning was very special (Wednesday). Jane and I talked for an hour before gym about motherhood, writing, letters et al. Rich conversation, rich connections. Ideas popping up from all directions. Afterwards, I began to think of the people I talk to and share with most comfortably, pleasurably, alivedly (just coined that one) and why this is so. Common to all of us, I think, is a finely tuned listening capacity, a feminist sensibility (with differences), a hungry curiosity about all things but especially human behaviour, and an enormous pleasure in making rich personal connections. Also political connections when they derive from real life, real experience, not merely cold, dispassionate intellectual critiques. The personal and political, the feeling and the thinking, the exchanging and the exploring, the joys and the

sorrows. My endless gratitude to the contemporary women's movement for opening me and other women up to these life-giving possibilities. Do women who have never been exposed to feminism begin to realize what they are missing or have missed? A kind of oxygen that lets you breathe and dream and come alive.

I alerted a young guy at the gym on a machine next to my mat that there were keys on the floor near him. Thought they might have slipped out of his pocket; it happens. He curtly responded he knew they were there. And me, I thought, why did I bother. Such a typical male response. I find many men are indifferent when I extend small gestures—like holding a door, or moving out of the way, or saying hello. Some older women might attribute this to age, white hair, ageism, etc. I don't! Just find many men to be unaware, unconscious, untouched by the "other," especially women. So they ignore small human gestures of caring. I guess in general men simply feel entitled. Something about being at the centre of things, rightfully, expecting nurturance from women (mothering) and allowed (as in adolescence) to be unresponsive, boorish when they don't care to extend themselves. Sort of like the men we see on TV these days, on all sides of the world, meeting together, fighting small or big wars, determining the fate of the rest of us on the planet. When will they ever learn?!?

November 14, 2001

I was sick with a rotten cold for four days this week and thus had to cancel yoga, massage, dinner with Rosemary (her birthday), etc., etc. I hate to have to cancel arrangements, to have my plans disrupted. But once stuck in the house, and if it's not too long a duration, I begin to enjoy the freedom of doing nothing,

going nowhere. It would never suit me as a lifestyle, but a periodic taste of it is very satisfying.

I loved our bridge non-bridge threesome the other day with you, me and Joan. Christel didn't want to risk catching whatever bug there might be in our house. Gil wasn't feeling so hot, and we thought he might be in for a bout of flu! So bridge was cancelled. Joan, however, didn't want to miss the gabbing and suggested having a cup of tea together. When I phoned to tell you our substitute plan, suggesting you might want to come, you leaped at the idea. And so we gabbed, checked in, you read your just published poems in the *Algonquin Roundtable Review*. I shocked both of you when I described going to sleep thinking of people I'm angry and upset with. It was a wonderful afternoon that flowed with unusual ease and authenticity. My kind of joy these days. Went to sleep last night thinking of the poem about your mother! Very moving!

Karen thinks Gil and I are unusual as parents in terms of our capacity for friendship and sharing. Says most of her friends' parents don't make these connections, sees it as a generational thing. Thinks her generation is more open, more connected.

Solange Chaput Roland died (*Dear Enemies* co-author). Said in the obituary that she was a pioneer in fighting for women's rights. I should have guessed! I was inspired by Nellie McClung's wholesome autobiographical stories (*Sowing Seeds in Danny* and *Clearing in the West*) long before I knew anything about suffragettes, feminism, the women's movement. Some chemistry draws me/drew me to the authors trying to tell women about themselves and the world. There are such remarkable undercurrents in all our psyches and the moments of revelation are just a glimpse of what lurks in

the unconscious. I was never a fan of psychoanalysis and Freud—
to put it mildly—but the existence of the unconscious, individual
and collective, has always resonated for me as part of the dynamic
of human behaviour. I particularly disliked the rationale of most
high-priced analysts who touted the argument that potential
"patients" would find money to pay their outrageous fees if they
were sufficiently motivated to get help.

Well, Gil had his hootenanny[24] last night at Botanica. Crowds
(to me) of people coming to sing all the old lefty and folk songs
and later even a few of the schmaltzy songs that you and I love.
This was Gil's night. I stay very separate and it works out for
both of us. He does what he wants, including who gets invited
and food and drinks. Before people arrive, I retreat to my
bedroom and rest. I emerge when things have gotten going and
gradually become part of the milieu. And enjoy. In my old age,
I'm not good with crowds, or people I hardly know, or singing
too many of the old songs about brotherhood and miners and
hoboes and sailors and wanderers and Abdul the bul-bul amir. I
tried getting everyone to sing "Sister, Carry On" (Womansing),
but it didn't really catch on. Someone else suggested "Singing for
our lives," meaning, I think, "We are gentle, angry women."
Which we did, except everyone but me sang "gentle, angry
people." And I thought, dammit, the whole evening is in the male
idiom, and then they have to take women out of this one song that's
about us. I didn't say anything, feeling it would be too mean-
spirited of me and no one was being malicious, just unconscious!

The music was great. A few guitars, a banjo (Mary), a harp

[24] folk song singalong popularized by Pete Seeger and the Weavers

(Pat), a double bass, one guy who played accordion and harmonica as well as guitars (Russ). Chris, Arthur. And two mandolins.

A very touching and meaningful part of the evening came from Pat. She's learning to play the harp as a vehicle for healing. Has breast cancer. With remissions and recurrences, she has decided to do no more chemo and radiation. Sister died of breast cancer. Is in a support group of breast cancer survivors. Had been studying palliative care and harp in U.S. program that sounds amazing, but it was very intense and demanding. The breast cancer recurred and she came home. Used to work for CUSO[25]. Spent five years in Cuba, speaks Spanish. One of many remarkable female social activists who gave her all.

Told how she was with one of the women in her support group a few hours before she died, playing the harp, holding her hand. You could have heard a pin drop. Gil reminded me today that Chris and Arthur, who lost partners to cancer, must have been thinking back to sad times. I was so overwhelmed by Pat herself that I, in typical single-minded fashion, related only to her.

Ruthie is great to have at these evenings. Belts it out, recalls words that no one else remembers (photographic memory, like my father).

I'm getting tickets to the *Vagina Monologues* in December for bridge group. And I've decided I'm going to treat. It's a birthday present for each of you because I always forget birthdays or I'm away for them, in Mexico. I'm delighted with the idea. Hope you are too, even though the timing is off.

[25] an international development organization

Hope your cold is better. Felt so comfortable when Christopher dropped over to pick up the bag he had left at the hootenanny. I was wearing thermal underwear, an ancient, droopy flannelette housecoat, not having brushed my teeth or combed my hair or bothered to pick up or organize anything from the total mess left from the party. Now that's friendship— we gabbed a short while, oblivious to appearances. At least Gil and I were. Nice! End of letter.

Lots of love,
Helen

Oonagh

Friday, October 26, 2001,
Mount Herbert Hotel, Dublin, 8 a.m.

Dearest Helen,

It is bliss to have a room of my own once more. I slept like a log. I bought myself a hot-water bottle yesterday and the bed, a whole double to myself, was so comfortable. I feel renewed and finally caught up on myself. No doubt Chris in Spain is feeling the same. Although we travel fairly well together, we are so used to having our space that all that togetherness is very tiring. Also this time we have moved about too much, so coming to Dublin is a bit like finding an oasis, without the sun! It poured yesterday but didn't stop me from walking the length of Bray Promenade. I was the only one there, and the waves were crashing against the shore. It was terrific, although I was very conscious that I was five minutes' walk away from Brian's house. I would love to have dropped in, but knew I couldn't. Anyway I enjoyed myself immensely, hopping on and off the DART, the commuter train that goes from one end of County Dublin along the coast to Greystones in County Wicklow—all of my old stomping ground.

In Dun Laoghaire, I stood in the small park overlooking the harbour. It was once my grandparents' orchard. The house

looked very warm and inviting. When my grandmother was alive, it was always like that. When she died, my grandfather didn't bother to look after it, so it never was the same for me. We had to move there for a number of years after we were forced to leave our home in Shankill. It was pretty awful as my grandfather didn't really want us there but felt he hadn't got much choice. My mother told me that if he hadn't, we probably would have gone into orphanages, at least Eithne and Niall would have.

Nine a.m. Decided to get some breakfast, as I didn't want to continue this stuff. One of the reasons I keep coming back to this hotel is the breakfast and the lovely room they serve it in overlooking a garden. It used to be a reasonable price, but it's pretty expensive now, and the service is not great. Still, it's just beside the station and I feel safe on my own. So, although I decide not to come here, I end up here anyway.

Today I go to visit June and Walter Kuhn, whom I met as friends of friends. So I will have lunch with them in their lovely home overlooking Dublin Bay, the same house that June grew up in. Guess where? Blackrock, where we lived for a number of years. June and Walter were both ballet dancers. I dearly love June and she me, and it's as if we have known each other for a thousand years. Walter considers me his third daughter! What a lovely chance meeting, eh? Like your friends in San Miguel.

After lunch today, they want to drive me to one of my favourite spots in the mountains, where June and I will walk, and Walter will wait for us in the car. He has a hernia and can't move very easily. Then this evening I will see Joe Fahey, my old boyfriend.

Oh, before I forget, June's home looks onto the back garden

of Desmond's family home (that's Desmond from Mallorca); can you keep up with it all? So I am looking forward to finding out more, although June is younger than Desmond by about six years. Desmond is seventy-eight. I have no doubt they knew each other, but because June has taken Walter's surname, Desmond hasn't heard of her. What a way of obliterating women's histories! I get so worked up about that. My mother's name was Marie Angela Farrell. I could change mine to Oonagh d'Angela; sounds better in French. I kept Berry, Edwin's family name, as I felt I had a better life with him than I did with my father's name O'Connor, and also I wanted the same name as my children, but I do get a bit resentful that we didn't consider O'Connor Berry in those days.

November 1, at home

I dearly wanted to post this from Ireland but just didn't manage to find that special quiet within myself that enables me to write my thoughts down. It isn't just a matter of external place, is it? Anyway, I'm back home, and delighted to be.

My dearest Helen, please never think you have to curtail your thoughts about death, dying, illness, whatever, with me. One of the great gifts my mother gave me during the last few weeks of her life was talking about her death, her fears, just her needing to talk about it all to me. There we were, two women chatting. I felt my mother recognized me as a mature woman, not her child daughter to be protected. Mind you, growing up in Ireland as a Catholic certainly helped my acceptance of death as a part of life. Over the years, Chris and I have written out what we want for our memorial services. Someone once said to me that I wanted control right up to the bitter end and beyond—true!

The day my mother was buried I planted primroses and violets. They come up every year and there is a primrose in bloom today in the garden. My mother loved her garden, planted lettuces, scallions and potatoes, and had one rosebush, which she loved. And then there's the lilac bush that David Pollock gave me a few years ago, and it's still alive and well, while he is in the Maycourt, very ill.

I want to continue with my Irish trip. I want to tell you a rather cute, funny story. I met up with my old, old boyfriend Joe Fahey. He was my boyfriend for about four years, beginning when I was eighteen. I left him to go to England, mainly because he couldn't make up his mind whether he wanted to marry me. A few years ago, I phoned him, and since then every time I go to Dublin, I see him. He is retired from the civil service and has a couple of radio shows on local radio—one is a music show and the other is interviewing older Dublin people about their lives. One of the things he and I used to do together was take bit parts in operas—I as a slave girl in *Aïda*, he as a soldier, etc., so music has been a big part of our past. He also was a great dancer, and we used to go dancing every week. Went to the races every week too, but that's another story. Anyway, over dinner in this rather posh Chinese restaurant, I asked him if he knew the tune to "Angels Guard Thee" and, guess what, in that crowded stuffy restaurant, he sang it to me, softly and gently in his very musical voice, very relaxed, as if this were the most natural thing in the world to do. What a magic moment, a memory I will not forget.

His family were extremely important to me when I was dating him. I met him at a dance and over the years became very much a part of his family. The thing that I remember most about

his mother and father was their amazing (at that time in Ireland) open house to all cultures and religions. His older sister, Eileen, died of a brain tumour twenty years ago. Joe and I used to go dancing in a club with a Jamaican all-steel band, and afterwards go back to their very tiny house on South Circular Road in Dublin, with whoever wanted to come. I remember Eileen having a major crush on a Jamaican guy called Vivian; he was gorgeous! Alma, Joe's younger sister, who now lives in London, Ontario, used to earn her pocket money by going down the street to the local synagogue to turn on lights on a Friday night. When Joe and I meet, we still talk about his parents, and how special they were, in a very quiet way, rather like Joe himself. His father used to bring me to hurling matches (do you know the game?) and the Abbey Theatre when Joe was away on trips for his work so that I wouldn't be lonely! They never spoke to me about my family, but I knew they knew it was very messy so they tried to make a small haven for me.

When Chris and I took Aaron over to Dublin a few years ago, Aaron said to me after meeting Joe, "Grandma, he is a very nice man!" He is that. I can't believe I've written so much about Joe. All I wanted to tell you was the little story about the song.

Saturday, November 3

I've just spoken to Paul, and I am totally stunned at what he said. I was telling him about my singing lessons and how I go around the house, up to the market, wherever, singing "Every Time We Say Goodbye." Dead silence from his end, then he said slowly, "Ma, this is amazing and strange, because every morning I go to Starbucks for a coffee, and as I walk I sing to Rachel "Every Time We Say Goodbye"!

Helen dearest, how about that for a connection? Sixth sense or what? When he told me, I burst into tears. Oh my God, I still can't believe it. Am I nuts to make such a big thing of this? Well, I'm nuts; I love it! Along with our letter writing, singing is becoming more and more important to me. I can't wait to start my lessons again next week. I just can't believe I had the courage to start lessons at my age when I can't read music.

Joe was very envious; he believes he should have been a singer. I agree—he has a very lovely voice. Paul has a terrific voice too. He has done a lot of public singing. I still don't know where his interest in the old tunes comes from as he sang folk. Helen, I have more or less decided not to sing with the choir. I don't feel good about the way I sing there. I don't like the building; I never have. Somehow the air is not good, and the overall surroundings do not turn me on. I also do not know any of the songs. What I really want to sing is the oldies. I wish there were a women's choir doing that. I am thinking of maybe joining the Orpheus Choir. They meet on a Friday night (not great) and I know if you don't want to sing in the musicals, you don't have to. I know the woman who plays piano for them. Anyway, what do you think? Maybe I'll be ready for a choir like Womansing in a year's time when I have had many lessons. Although having said that, I don't think I'm interested enough!

I can't believe how long this letter is; and it not only spans time but place too. I think I write better in the kitchen when Chris is out. I watch the birds outside; a cardinal keeps coming back to the bird feeder.

Helen, my dear, I so enjoyed yesterday with you and Joan. All that great talk about memory; I loved it.

Anyway, I have now reached my writing limit for today. God, I feel so passionate about it that I become exhausted after a while and need to get up and go for a long walk.

Much love to your dear self, Helen. I sometimes have to pinch myself to believe it's true that we are writing to each other in this marvellous, open way.

Oonagh xxx

Oonagh

Saturday, November 17, 2001, 11 a.m.

Dearest Helen,

Well, I've just pulled myself together after talking with Gil about whether I was going to the demonstration. I feel totally burnt out, so any suggestion that I should be doing anything more than I am sends me into despair. When I say burnt out, I mean on a global scale: I can't respond, not even when it's on my own doorstep. It took talking and reacting to what Gil said to make me fully aware of why my body is so tired, why I want to sing (more about that later), why I want to write to you and also why the idea of leaving Amethyst becomes less and less appealing. That is the place where I do my work, politically and personally; that is the place where it all comes together.

I wonder if Gil realizes that spending five minutes with a woman at Amethyst is as political a statement as marching in a rally, if not more so! I don't mean to single out Gil, but our conversation this a.m. really started me thinking; that, and my fury that no country gave a damn about the women of Afghanistan and still doesn't; and, on a local level in Ottawa, that people marginalize women and the work we do with each other.

So, dearest Helen, I'd be somewhat out of touch with my reality and the women of the world if I didn't think and feel the way I do. I hear your "Yes, Oonagh" loud and clear; and every word I write to you and that you write to me is our political statement, right? I'm sure this comes out as if I were sure of what I say. I'm not, Helen. I'm confused and trying very hard to make sense of myself, and what I'm about at this moment in time.

Tuesday, November 20

Well, isn't this great, Helen. Three days later and the thoughts in my head have changed somewhat in that, after a confusing board meeting last night at Amethyst, I'm ready to quit *now*! I am a great actor at work. I pretend I have a lot of energy when I haven't, and the constant activity and noise at work causes anxiety in me. I sigh with relief when I arrive home to the peace and quietness. At present I have a very big caseload. Most of the women are active, meaning they are attending meetings on a regular basis. On top of my caseload, I am on committees and the board, and my hours are seventeen and a half hours a week! Just writing about it causes anxiety. Putting this down on paper reminds me that before I went on holidays, I said I was giving it another few months, until January 2002, in fact, and then I would make up my mind. I do think I have already decided, but it is proving very difficult. We hired another counsellor in September, and she is going on maternity leave in December. That is putting great stress on everyone. I was hoping my holiday would have helped and that I would go back to Amethyst renewed and refreshed. But within a week, I found myself getting exhausted physically and mentally. I am bordering on burnout locally as well as globally.

Dearest Helen, I hope you don't mind me sorting myself out here. Writing about it helps me cut through my denial of how I really feel and what I have to do soon! I feel so blessed that I have a cozy, comfortable home, a sunny room of my own; enough money to buy comforts (I shouldn't feel blessed—all of that should be the right of every human being); my friends; writing and singing; and last but not least, my children, who all seem to be at peace with me (today!). Leaving Amethyst is like leaving a relationship. After twenty-two years of intensive community, I am scared and fearful of the void it will leave in me. Since I was sixteen years of age, I have worked inside and outside the home, plus giving time to theatre work, political stuff, chaplaincy work (with the Unitarian Church), sports, etc. When I think back on my talk with Gil, what I would have loved him to have said when I mentioned my work at Amethyst was "Oonagh, that is enough work for anyone to do." And, Helen, I need to say that to myself, because whatever I do or have done never seemed to be enough; proving myself to myself and others; believing the facade that others have helped create for me and that I have found so rewarding at times and so totally exhausting. Chris was shocked when we first began living together by my need for a room of my own, a precondition to our living together; my lack of enthusiasm for any form of entertaining; my constant complaining if we went out to dinner with others more than once a month; my point-blank refusal to have anyone stay with us, except for kids and Aaron. So the charming, interested (always interested in others!), energetic woman turned into a very private, somewhat solitary person behind closed doors. The funny thing is that Chris also needs space and quiet to think his own thoughts, and recently he

has admitted this, although he still loves meeting new people, going to parties and is always game for travel and spur-of-the-moment encounters. And, yes, I do like meeting people, but on my terms. Although Chris talks about the work I do at Amethyst as demanding and exhausting, he isn't very happy when I remind him of that fact, and it's interfering with our social life. I think he believes if I leave, things will be a little different; dream on there, Chris!

Tuesday, November 20, 7:30 p.m.

I'm in my favourite spot at the kitchen table; Chris is out at some travel movie about South America, so I have the place to myself. I can't see the river as it's so dark, but I know it's there. My moods are up and down like a yo-yo these days. None of my clients showed up today, for one reason or another, so I managed to catch up on paperwork, which I hate with a passion, and it wasn't so hectic there today. I spoke to Susan Ford last night, and she told me that Womansing has joined with In Harmony, as neither of them had enough women to make a choir; now there are thirty-six women! I would have felt a lot better with a bigger choir, as I could have hidden behind some of the better singers. Oh well. I am very satisfied with the folklore choir so far. Hey, I've been to only one practice. I like the energy, love the mixture of ages and think the director is amazing. What did I do before I sang? It has become so very important to me, and my get-togethers with Anna are better than any therapy session. I am now learning "Blue Moon," and I would love to be able to sing "Memory" from *Cats*. I have big dreams, haven't I?

Last week, I went to the Maycourt Hospice to visit our friend

David Pollock. During the war he was posted to England, where he worked on radar, and during his off-duty hours played jazz piano in the pubs. He gave it up for many years, and then went back to it in his late sixties. I sat with him last week, holding his hand and telling him that he was one of the most attractive and interesting men I had ever met, and then I sang to him "Every Time We Say Goodbye." Do you now think I am crazy, Helen? It was lovely for me, and he smiled and squeezed my hand. He was the rare man who asked questions and seemed really interested; he always remembered what I said to him! Chris and I met him and Sheila at Adela's and became friends. We went to movies and ate out at different restaurants with them—it was a very easy going friendship. Maybe Sheila will play bridge with us one day. She plays a lot, and seems to have a group of women friends that she meets for lunch, etc., like you, like me.

Joyful was the word that came to mind as I read the article you're going to send to "Facts and Arguments." You managed to convey the essence of our letter writing; amazing. I can imagine turning to the back page of the paper and seeing this terrific piece that will speak to all the Luddites across the country. Seriously, Helen, it bubbles with life and you.

Well, my dearest friend, I can't believe I actually have written so many pages. I think this is the first time I have used our CP to express so much anxiety and confusion and pain. No doubt it won't be the last!

> With much love and continued gratitude at
> what we are about,

Oonagh xxx

Helen

Sunday, November 18, 2001, 6 p.m.

My dear Oonagh,

You say you write better in the kitchen when Chris is out. For me, it's in the living room when Gil is out or away. I drove him to the airport this morning to catch a plane to Vancouver to attend the CUPE convention. He loves being back at conventions amid the swirling tensions and conflicts, the personalities and opposing sides leading up to the elections, the hot issues, the suspense re outcomes. The adversaries at the top are Judy Darcy (president) and Geraldine McGuire (secretary/treasurer). They used to work well together, but at some point a few years ago there was a rift and the women have hardly spoken since. I'll be rooting for Judy, who has worked hard for women in and beyond CUPE.

Then Gil goes to Hawaii for a week. And in December, California to visit his friend Arthur. I have not one ounce of envy. My world in Ottawa—other than San Miguel and short jaunts elsewhere—is big enough for me. Gil did acknowledge that he was travelling a lot because he realizes there could be limitations in years to come that will restrict his freedom to travel. Rather

wistfully, he commented that I seem to be finished with visiting places other than Mexico. True, I said, except for always having had a yen to see Greece or Spain. So now he is suggesting we go to either of these countries next year!

You and I talked by phone about your joining the demonstration protesting the actions of the G20 finance ministers meeting this weekend in Ottawa. How you wandered down to Rideau and Sussex, saw the riot police with dogs and tear gas and God knows what else, visualized a police state and then could not stay away from the march. I was very moved by your struggle—with yourself, in relation to world events, how and why you decided to move from being observer to participant.

It is different for me. I seem to have given up on marching, demonstrating. And at present, I have too many conflicting feelings re all the macro political issues. Besides, the core of me, the committed me remains almost exclusively invested in addressing the oppression of women, individually and collectively. Call me narrow, call me blind, call me limited—that is where my heart and soul remain.

I've lost my credibility re predicting behaviour among the Levines. I simply assumed Gil and Ruthie would go on the march this weekend. Didn't even discuss it. I would not, and they would. A given. To my surprise, Gil remained at home. Said he was too busy getting ready for his trips and hadn't been involved in all the preparatory stuff. I was blown away. I liked the fact that there was a glimpse of a shift in his political behaviour. Karen and I humorously, and I sometimes not so humorously, refer to him as the Stalinist in the family.

Then Ruthie came over and bluntly and directly announced

that she wasn't about to expose herself to tear gas and gave me a few other reasons for her decision. This from my very committed and responsible daughter. Though I love in her and others this committed way of being in the world, I was overjoyed to know that she could and would diverge from the "conventional" wisdom or the politically correct positions of the labour movement or the left. Ruthie isn't characteristically blunt, so her decision signalled to me a toughening-up, more clarity. My guess is that struggles with Daniel at home have contributed to this development. God, it's amazing, and oh, so painful, the stories of how we parents learn unwillingly but inevitably from our growing kids.

My classic story about learning from teenage kids is how in the late '60s Ruthie was home from Glendon College,[26] lolling around, doing nothing in particular. I was all involved in a march and rally on Parliament Hill around the right to abortion. Ruthie was (or seemed to be) totally indifferent, clearly uninterested in joining the demonstration. I was furious, she was immovable. I could not believe or accept the fact that my daughter didn't give a damn about abortion (my "then" interpretation). Much later, I realized that growing kids unconsciously or consciously perceive what's nearest and dearest to your heart and then go in the opposite direction. For a time, shorter or longer. They have to, to establish themselves as separate persons. A most profound lesson for parents, one most of us avoid learning as long as we can.

Strange, this episode comes back to me just when Ruthie

[26] part of York University in Toronto

again departs from family norms. What on earth is going on with the Levines these days?

November 19

Went to the fitness centre with Jane, who had been on the march on Saturday. Her experience was similar to yours, reacting to the overwhelming police presence, the dogs, etc. She was nearby when a reporter was whacked by a cop. He told the cop he was a reporter and was whacked a second time. She found the experience scary but was glad to be there. Said most of the people she knows who you would expect to be demonstrating were not present. Why? She thinks it's fear of police violence. Jane felt she was there re her/our right to dissent, how that right is now much endangered. By the police, by the state, by the impending new legislation re terrorism that will take away all kinds of civil rights.

The other person who marched, second time in his life, was Shirley's partner, Henry. He too had seen the riot police and responded by participating. Reminds me of summer 1968 when the Levines (all four of us) were in Paris, France. Tremendous political ferment, everything and everyone on strike (taxis, high schools, theatres, factories, universities) and riot police were everywhere. Paris has special riot squads known to be brutal and armed to the teeth. Who ever imagined we might someday have our Canadian version?

The dinner the other night, with about ten people, was a throwback to the '50s. Guys taking up all the space, women silent or filling in with questions or brief comments, no one interested in knowing anything about anyone else. Most of it impersonal

talk that passes for conversation. I wanted to scream, watched Gil being Mr. Friendly and laughing at some of the pathetic "jokes." My face gives it all away, always has, but I honestly don't know what to do with said face in these situations.

All I can say is that men need to leave it to women to make social get-togethers viable and inclusive. Meanwhile, remind me not to do this again. I could have stayed home. Gil could have gone to dinner.

I loved your story about you and Paul and singing "Every Time We Say Goodbye." What a meeting of hearts and souls via music, with your *own kid*. The mysterious, rich connections that get made unconsciously. When we used to bike a lot, over long distances, I would find myself humming a song, any old song. It somehow connected with what I was seeing or thinking or feeling. I loved those long, quiet stretches of biking, mostly in the countryside, feeling so healthy, so free in the space all around us. Riding a bicycle, drinking in the fresh air, hair blowing in the wind, cheeks glowing with wind and sun—that always signified freedom to me. And so it was for women in the nineteenth century when they first took to bicycles. It meant they were riding on their own, steering their own course, starting and stopping when they chose. Joan Taylor from Wheelwomen of Canada wrote a paper on this for a women's studies course—the connection between the bicycle and women's liberation!

I really wanted to write you about my time in Toronto recently. It was a trip that came full circle, rewarding from start to finish. Memorable. Karen nurtured me in all the ways that matter—I felt very much loved and cared for. I spent some time with Gabriel, watched him have a tennis lesson. He's a whiz at six. Responsive

and interesting. Hope it lasts. Whatever happens, this kid has a good, solid foundation that should see him through his inevitable growing-up struggles.

Karen and I, her feminist friends, Talin and Margie, and Donna and Gwen were together at Doris Anderson's eightieth birthday bash at the Royal York. It was a stupendous event, organized with imagination, substance, fun and music. Close to fifteen hundred people were seated at pre-selected tables of ten in two large dining rooms with huge video screens, some speakers live in one room, some in the other. Sounds like a recipe for disaster. But it wasn't. CBC's Shelagh Rogers was emcee; Governor General Adrienne Clarkson, who once was a *Chatelaine* columnist, spoke at length with warmth, wit and an outspoken feminist perspective (what a GG!); Mary Lou Fallis, opera singer, sang a funny love song for Doris; and much, much more. Program was interspersed with delicious food. Doris spoke in that understated, dry, ironic way she has—must be taking voice lessons, voice much improved—and took us back through the highs and lows of the women's movement as well as sharing personal tidbits.

The atmosphere in our dining room was electric, full of fun, laughter, nostalgia and inspiration. We jumped up and down for standing ovations; it was as if the women's movement were still very much alive. No one seemed to be worried about covering all the bases of political correctness. It was an outpouring of spontaneity and storytelling. I'm not so naïve as to believe it could have been completely simple and straightforward, but I didn't care. It was sheer joy and our small group had a ball.

Doris looks lovely at eighty. She always, from way back,

refers to her own messes and mistakes, which especially endears her to me and probably many other women.

I felt very proud to be there, only wished I had dragged Ruthie with me. Met a handful of women I had known. Also a doctoral student at OISE[27] who has read all my stuff (that's always a thrill!).

In Toronto I saw Frances and Ida, two old friends from my left wing, United Jewish Peoples Order days in Toronto, both social workers. Frances is eighty-four, Ida my age. Ida has been caretaking her 103-year-old father for the past few years. Until a few weeks ago he managed on his own, with her unwavering support, in his own apartment.

Am reading Barbara Ehrenreich's *Nickel and Dimed: On (Not) Getting By in America*. I think you would like it. Not great literature but gutsy reporting, with humour—close to the bone. About her year-long experience posing as a low-paid, unskilled woman in different wretched jobs, where many women spend their working lives.

My God, I'm up to page ten of this letter. Enough already. My shoulders ache, my ass is sore, my fingers (right hand) are rubbed thin. So much for handwriting.

I think you're much more comfortable with men than I am, I'm jealous of your visits with the old boyfriend in Ireland. My first love has forsaken or forgotten me, but then I don't contact him. I left him when he didn't want to be my own true love forever and ever. Then I moaned around for a year at Queen's, singing "None but the Lonely Heart" and weeping.

[27] Ontario Institute for Studies in Education

See you for lunch on Saturday. What on earth will we talk about! Jane suggested that in my piece on letters I comment about why we write even though we meet and talk, and phone and talk. Good point.

With much love to you, Oonagh, partly because you too have a passion for letters. We *have* discovered America.

Helen

Oonagh

Sunday, December 2, 2001, 10 a.m.

Dearest Helen,

Here I am again, in the kitchen, looking out over the river, knowing I only have a short time with you, as Chris went out for a brief visit to the Xerox machine at Carleton. However, he has a poetry group meeting this afternoon, so I will be back. I continue to be all over the place; one hour loads of energy, the next hour physically exhausted and wanting to lie down. I went to the doctor a few weeks ago and got blood tests, etc., which didn't show up anything. I do feel I have some sort of low-grade virus, which is affecting me physically, aside from my ups and downs around Amethyst.

One day I decide to leave at the end of January, the next day I decide the end of March. So in some ways I have made my decision to leave, but I'm still not sure when. I have made an appointment with someone at the CPP[28] office, so that by Thursday I will have to decide the dates. Of course, I can always cancel the appointment. A colleague suggested I go on disability

[28] Canada Pension Plan

for three to five months and then decide if I want to leave. In actual fact, that was a helpful suggestion because it made me think ahead to six months down the road, and I know if I took the time off, I would not want to return. That is definitely not an option for me, aside from the awful hassle with insurance companies. So, dearest Helen, I'll keep you posted on my up-and-down "I'll do it/I won't do it" plans. I do know that I want to leave Amethyst knowing that my work is still good and that I will be missed for it by the women I work with each day and by my colleagues.

A few days ago, one of my new colleagues told me that I was fantastic in facilitating groups and workshops. I was so shocked that I burst into tears. Although, over the years, I have consistently had great yearly evaluations, it is very rare for me to hear praise for individual tasks. It's as if my younger colleagues do not know that we older ones need reassurance too. I have certainly tried to talk to them about my lack of confidence in presenting material at workshops, in particular the ones that I haven't done before, and it's as if they don't want to hear and somehow don't believe me. The workshop that the new counsellor witnessed was one I have done for years, and I love doing it, but even with that one I spent most of last Tuesday morning at home, going over and over the material until I could have done it in my sleep.

I have very important letters to write and songs to sing! I think the problem for me around workshops is that I have to believe in the material I am presenting, but nowadays I question it all. The way I survive is to turn them into discussion groups, which is much more me. I even suggested that we stop calling them workshops and instead call them discussion groups, but

most of my colleagues don't want that. Yet most of them agree that input from the women is of the utmost importance. You know, Helen, I don't think we are attentive enough to the language we use.

A few months ago we had a young woman from the Women's Studies program in the ten-day program, which has many workshops in it. At the end of the ten days she gave us a scathing evaluation of our workshops—said none of us knew how to run them, and we needed training. Needless to say, we were all pretty upset but managed to rationalize by saying that ten other women liked what we did. But I think if we called them discussion groups we wouldn't set ourselves up to be compared with a university style set-up. What do you think?

Helen, I keep thinking of your essay. I hope they—the *Globe*'s "Facts and Arguments" editors—get in touch soon, like this week, and publish it before you take off for San Miguel. I am so excited about it. Imagine that when we decided to write our letters, we said we weren't going to tell anyone except immediate family. Well, talk about "think globally, act locally"! You have reversed that saying, or done something to it, anyway. "Act and think locally and globally"—way to go, Helen! I think there will be a number of women who will read the essay and say yes to it. You should consider asking for royalties from Canada Post. What did your writing group think of it?

I seem to be very stuck with my other writings these days. Nothing creative comes to mind, although I do have a little spark that keeps coming back. And during the funeral service for David Pollock, it was mentioned how he would close his eyes, and imagine the little town of Kinistino where he grew up, and

he also remembered all the people who lived there and in recent years began writing to a friend of his from way back, so they shared their memories of this little town. I have often thought of writing a sort of *Under Milk Wood* version of Shankill. Like David, I too can remember, in detail, the living that went on in that village. I remember spending a lot of time looking out of the bedroom window, and when not doing that, I listened in to conversations. And in a small village in Ireland, lots of gossip and strange happenings went on. Maybe one day, the spark will turn into a flame and I'll manage to do something with it.

God, I'm hopping and skipping all over the place with this, in my usual way, eh? When I began writing this letter this a.m., I thought I was going to grumble about my older son, Niall, whom for the most part I enjoy and yack to on a weekly basis. Since he left Ottawa when he was twenty-two or twenty-three, he has always phoned me on a regular basis, but there are certain topics, such as my financial status, where he oversteps his boundaries or my boundaries.

Over the years, I have stupidly brought up minor concerns about pensions, and somehow what he hears is that I am worried about money and he becomes extremely opinionated. Yesterday I spoke to him about the idea of retiring, and before I knew what had hit me, we were discussing my pension. Talk about getting sidetracked! I was so angry at myself for allowing that to happen. I did cut him off, but it certainly left a bad feeling in me. So, dear Helen, I've had my grumble about Niall!

You know, Helen, I have more "evil" thoughts around my children than I have about anyone else. Does that surprise you? I know it comes from a place of deep hurt. I often say in group to

the women, that yes, as mothers we may have to say sorry to our children, but they also have to say sorry to us! Good enough mothers, that's what we are, given that we never got the chance to write the job description. I think the reason why my mother and I got on so well during the last years of her life was the fact that we talked with each other about our hurts. Not that we went into it all in great detail, we just sort of said sorry to each other and began to build an equal loving relationship based on our obvious admiration, love and respect for each other. Slowly but surely it's getting there with my Helen. I have always felt respect from her but mother/daughter/grandmother roles caused a lot of anxiety and friction. Now that Aaron is eighteen, I feel that, at last, Helen and I can get on with a relationship that had to be put on hold for all these years. She didn't leave Ottawa, but she certainly moved away from me to deal with her life as a mother. I think it's amazing how we came through it all and didn't kill each other in the process. On the other hand, I have a very different type of relationship with Niall and Paul. I laugh a lot with Niall—we have a camaraderie sort of relationship, and I can imagine myself doing things with him such as sailing or motor biking—he is a terrific driver. Paul on the other hand is intense and shares my love of theatre and writing. He is the child I talk about my writing to, and he is the one who shows interest in it. I hope he gets back to his own writing one day. There is nothing superficial about my relationship with Paul. He would not tolerate that.

Tuesday, December 4

Dribs and drabs again, dearest Helen. Once more at the kitchen table, but Chris is upstairs. So I banned him from the

kitchen under pain of death. Bossy, eh? It's 11 a.m. and I don't have to be at work until 4 p.m. and there are now rumblings of racism at Amethyst. One of my colleagues has been accused of making a racist remark to another colleague and it looks as if the shit has hit the fan big time. The union and the board have been notified and the woman who has made the accusation says she is going to hire a lawyer. I'll keep you posted on what's happening. Sigh! Sigh! I am so relieved I am not the union steward and I am so relieved that I have decided to leave and leave I will, probably earlier than later, as I cannot and will not go through yet another crisis. It's as if we never manage to get to the root causes which have plagued us since day one. Maybe our hopes and dreams for the place were totally unrealistic from the start. Maybe it's something to do with our collective insecurities as women, thanks to the thousands of years of oppression, maybe it's our personalities, maybe it's all of the above! Who knows, all I know is that I can't wait to leave.

I now have to go and prepare snacks for the annual Amethyst party which is tonight. Can you imagine having to smile and be pleasant when all hell is breaking loose under the surface? Thank God for my acting skills.

Much love dear friend,
Oonagh xxx

P.S. What a mean short letter!

Helen
December 2, 2001

My dear Oonagh,

It's Sunday morning at seven-thirty. Had a good sleep, not something I ever take for granted. Gil comes back today from Hawaii. I've liked being on my own, having the house to myself. Gil has enjoyed being away. When he last phoned he said he could stay a few extra days—likes the sun, the tennis, the film festival, etc. We two are so in sync these days about separateness and differences; hard to believe because these same questions used to be explosive.

I was fascinated by what you last wrote re exhaustion, image, need for privacy, being solitary behind closed doors, lack of enthusiasm for any form of entertaining—"so the charming, interested (always interested in others!) energetic woman turned into a very private, somewhat solitary person behind closed doors." Beautifully expressed, Oonagh, including the point about how rewarding the image can be. Rings bells for me. Except I think of the different parts of me that look contradictory—the active, energetic, involved and friendship-oriented me, and then the solitary, daydreaming, needing-to-be-quiet-and-alone me.

What happens, I guess, is that others experience us much more in the public sphere, and no matter how much we disclose of the other parts of the self, they aren't visible or easily understood. Probably why people who listen a lot (i.e., women) tune in on a different wavelength to what human beings are really all about. I think you and I are quite similar in these ways, and perhaps our CP helps us integrate the public and private parts of ourselves. Writing letters, a solitary, reflective, private activity, lends itself to all kinds of storytelling about our external worlds, our activism, our involvements, our social interactions.

Friendships have always been profoundly important to me, in their presence or absence or complexities, in joy or in sorrow. They (the closer ones) somehow make things possible for me. I don't seem to function without them. In general, I'm more autonomous and self-sufficient in my old age than ever before in my life. A late, very late, bloomer for sure. But intellectually and emotionally, I need other people, close and caring, to help ignite my thinking and my passions. And *initiative*. I'm such a stereo-typical second child, as a kid dominated and controlled by an older sibling. The old patterns are never completely extin-guished, but they do finally recede, if you're lucky, leaving a more authentic human being free to emerge. Of course, all this is the stuff of counselling and human potential. And why it's useless to try working with others unless you've faced and worked on and with your own garbage. My friend Eva and I, in our secret mutual admiration society, used to think we were the only two in the whole wide world who truly understood the process of change. A slight case of megalomania. Would you like to be admitted to this select/elite/delusional society, dead or alive?!

"Forget your perfect offering. There is a crack in everything. That's how the light gets in"—from "Anthem" by Leonard Cohen. The song was mentioned in an essay on perfectionism by June Grant on CBC Radio's *Sunday Edition*, then played afterwards. I love, absolutely love, Sunday radio. I even listened to Dr. Patricia Baird and some guy named Bernstein (Health Canada?) on cloning. Mostly I turn off re science/scientists. At this stage of evolution, I think we need to spend a long time developing sane human behaviours before wasting resources on space or cloning or Mars or bombs and missiles. But I must admit the discussion was an interesting and thoughtful exploration of cloning and the commodification of human life.

I have so much to write about. I am thrilled to have sent the essay on handwritten letters and our CP to "Facts and Arguments" in the *Globe and Mail*. For years, I have read the essay on the back page of the front section of the *Globe* first thing in the morning, plus "Lives Lived" beside it. I invariably wish I had written the good pieces and feel I could have. Essays are my chosen medium. I've written them for years in my free-fall writing group but never took it the one step further. Submitting was a dream, a wish, a hope—no more. My lack of initiative re the practical side of writing kept me from acting on the simplest of concrete details in submitting my stuff anywhere. What I've had published in the past are pieces I wrote on request and finished because patient feminist editors pushed, helped, waited, encouraged and finally did all the practical stuff.

So what happened this time? Firstly, Susan from our writing group moved to Whitehorse, and before she left bluntly told the remaining three of us that we'd better get our act together and

take our writing more seriously. We dropped the free-falls. Jane submitted an article to *The Citizen* on public garden plots and urban development. It was accepted. Faith's work toward a memoir of growing up in Thunder Bay is slowly but inexorably moving toward a book. She writes exquisitely. And now me submitting to the *Globe*.

Yes, Oonagh, tell me my piece is great; shades of Eva who thought likewise of our co-written story about friendship. It got rejected by *Canadian Woman Studies* for an issue on women and aging, later was published in *Spider Women*, an anthology. Karen liked my essay on letters. I read it to her over the phone. However I know I can make my material sound infinitely more interesting when I speak. The upshot is that I'm not so sure the essay is good enough. I know the topic is interesting, I know what you and I are doing is more than interesting, but I don't know if the piece is cohesive, if it flows as it should or could. If it is rejected, I will hopefully rewrite and resubmit to the *Globe* or elsewhere because I do love the story of you and me and our beloved CP.

We've talked in so many ways about friends and friendship. I want to say how significant your friendship was/is in taking me by the hand, step by step, through the practicalities of submitting this piece to "Facts and Arguments." You even offered to send it in for me (at lunch, remember?), and I refused, knowing I have to initiate at least a few small steps re writing and submitting. So I wrote a cover letter, addressed the envelope and put it in the mailbox. I even loved my cover letter, thought it was hilarious when I dreamed up: "Helen Levine hopes to become a writer. Time is short."

But you, dear friend, put it on your computer, more than once added, deleted, suggested, reacted. That whole weekend, you orchestrated our comings and goings, the consultations with Christopher, the phone calls, the reminders about sticking to rules re numbers of words. You encouraged and also challenged me a bit (my obsession with endless editing). And Christopher came and went with the printouts so things kept moving and the momentum was sustained. Thank you both a lot for all of this.

I'm brimming over with stuff to tell you about. I'm beginning to realize why real writers live solitary lives. There just isn't enough time or space in an ordinary life to deal with the jumble of stories, ideas, experiences, connections that jump around in one's head. Is this partly why you are thinking of retirement? I get very mixed up when you write about your ambivalence. On the one hand, I think it must add so much to your life to be working in personal/political ways in a feminist service. You are really the elder (Sandy seems younger; is she?) who carries the history of the place, of its achievements, conflicts and dilemmas. On the other hand, I remember well when I no longer wanted to teach and retired at sixty-four. Much later I gave up feminist counselling, which I had loved but also no longer wanted to do.

Two happenings this week stand out for me. One was the launch of Anna Heilman's memoir. She was in Auschwitz between thirteen and fifteen years of age, saved gunpowder to help blow up one of the crematoria and saw her older sister and three other young women publicly hanged for the "crime." Wanted to die, wanted to not go on living. Was literally saved by her sister's friend Martha, who somehow found her a pair of shoes and dragged her on the death march from Auschwitz.

The title of Anna's book is *Never Far Away*, subtitled *The Auschwitz Chronicles of Anna Heilman*. I love the picture of the three sisters on the cover and feel pure hatred for the Nazis. Despite Anna's horrifying life and death experiences and terrible losses, she herself has never seemed bitter or angry and said as much at the launch. It's as though her experience took her somewhere beyond any emotions that can be put into words. At the launch, she read a bit from her book, told some stories, answered questions (they kept coming) and I think gave all of us the gift of herself, past and present. I got the sense of an authentic, blunt and brave human being who emerged from hell and has lived a rich life. I was stunned listening to her, watching her, grasping in only a limited way what she was trying to tell us.

I feel inadequate with language right now. But I'll plod on. Anna's daughter intervened at one point (she has two daughters) to explain how her mom used to tell her children, "You have only one life; we all die, so don't let your fears rule you and prevent you from living that one life to the fullest." She also made the point several times that we don't hear many stories of women and the Holocaust. She had always felt her sister and the other three young women who risked their lives stealing gunpowder from the munitions factory where they worked had died in vain. Now, with publication of the book, she feels perhaps it wasn't all in vain. Much of the book is based on the journal she wrote in Polish after the war. She never wanted to look at it again. But the same friend, Martha, who now lives in Belgium, visited and insisted that the journal be translated.

Oonagh, you're going to hear a lot from me about Jews, being Jewish, the rampant anti-Semitism that I see in the world, how

the criticism of Israel is often, consciously or unconsciously, used to criticize all Jews, to promote the historic scapegoating that has haunted us over the centuries. It feels as though the Holocaust is sometimes deemed merely an incident, a moment in history, and thus easily diminished.

I had an experience with Jane at the gym last Friday. We were on the bicycles, gabbing. Can't recall her exact words. The subject of Israel came up. At some point I said, "What you're saying is really dangerous." She continued. I repeated what I had said earlier, definitively. I felt my throat tighten and tears well up (not visibly) and somehow ended the conversation. I trust Jane's world view and personal integrity and we will continue the dialogue soon. But I was shocked and surprised by my own reaction. There's more buried in me than I've realized, and post-September 11, it's rising to the surface, to consciousness.

What happened afterwards, as I lay on the mat doing my stretches, was a vivid recall of experiences from childhood and youth, of anti-Semitism. My best friend on the street; my teacher at Glebe Collegiate; my classmate at a summer government job before going to Queen's. And then I thought of *Hana's Suitcase*, how the Bradys were the only Jews in the town, how friends became nonfriends. Oh God, Oonagh, the loaded connections between anti-Semitism and friendship! It's as though all the nerve endings in my very being have been alerted to danger.

And today, suicide bombers striking three times in Israel, the killings, the God-knows-how-awful injuries. The report that Bobby Fischer (chess genius) is celebrating September 11. The neo-Nazis marching in a Jewish neighbourhood in Germany.

Gil will be home tonight. I'll be glad to see him. And I'll see Jane at the gym in the morning; we have to explore whatever happened and try to understand what got so tangled up for me. Christel is home; enjoyed Cuba. Rachel is thriving in Nepal; we're all proud of her guts, her sense of adventure.

With much love,
Helen

Oonagh

December 16, 2001, 6 a.m.

Dearest Helen,

I tossed and turned all night, what with a bad cold, my head pounding, and thinking of Amethyst, so I decided not to try getting back to sleep again but to write. I am definitely not thinking clearly, so God knows how this letter will read, and I also need to read your last letter again, as there were things I wanted to respond to, but my entire life seems to have been put on hold with the Amethyst crisis, yet again. At least this time I am not the central figure. I can't tell you, Helen, how very relieved I am that I am leaving. Certainly the decision was difficult to make, but once it was made, the relief was immense.

Nine a.m. Took an intermission break for coffee and my morning chat with Chris. Today was good as we both were gentle with each other, knowing that neither of us is 100 percent. I do love our early morning coffee and talk, but sometimes I just don't want to be bothered, and that's a problem. Chris is always in good humour in the morning. He wakes up very early, so that by the time I go down for my coffee, he has been awake for hours. Mostly I just want my coffee and the newspaper. After

that, I'm ready to talk or fight! But whatever way it comes out, I do love the ritual of it all.

I think I told you that when Chris was in India for twelve weeks, I replaced our chats with writing to him each day and then posted a letter at the end of each week to some unknown destination that he was heading to. He managed to get all of my letters. A number of years ago, I collected all his letters to me and my letters to him and thought of sending them to a publisher, but he wasn't too keen. Can't remember why; I must ask him again. I remember when I began rereading them, how exotic and exciting his descriptions of his travels were, and how focused mine were on the daily tasks of routine; I loved the contrast. I still think they would make an interesting book. Maybe I'll get back to them, after ours is published. I think we should call it *Keep the Home Fires Burning*!

Helen, I will miss you when you go to Mexico. Already, I'm beginning to have withdrawal signs. Because of our letter writing, I feel our friendship, be it by phone, or yacking over lunch, or playing bridge, has become more intense and intimate. I think the big difference for me is that as we write and share our innermost thoughts, our contradictions, our joys and sorrows and evil thoughts, I know that I do not have to explain myself to you. I trust you, and I trust myself with you. You have always been a very dear friend, and I remember feeling delighted when we finally met in friendship. And now, I believe we have taken another major step on our path to becoming "soul mates." I hope that doesn't frighten you to death. I fly with my feet firmly planted on the ground.

I hope, dear friend, you have now realized that I am avoiding

the "A" problem. It feels so good not to think about it. Yesterday and Friday, although I didn't feel well, I was so agitated about the place that I painted a wall all the way up one flight of stairs. I think it looks great, and doing it released the physical tension in my body and allowed me to think about things. When Dr. Mary Alice Henry asked me how I was going to cope with my stress, I told her I was going to paint a wall. Her answer: "Whatever turns you on, Oonagh."

Thursday, December 20, 8:30 a.m.

I never pray, but today, this morning, when I woke up I prayed for wisdom, for understanding and for the grace to "tip-toe through the tulips" with dignity and compassion, so that there will be no major repercussions for Amethyst.

Today—I hope—is our final meeting with the union, board and griever. She has asked me to attend the meeting as she feels that I would be objective (I'm not sure about that!), fair and supportive (I hope to be). I can't go into everything that has happened over the past week. There was an emergency board meeting, which went on for hours. Thank God for Linda Advocaat and Diane Weber,[29] both of whom were very supportive of the staff; plus Diane has loads of knowledge around human rights issues in the workplace.

December 20, 4 p.m.

What an exhausting, painful meeting for us all. But at least I think it has finally been resolved. Not to anyone's satisfaction,

[29] board members

but at least we hope that we can live with it. In the end it came down to Anne Hrnchiar[30] (bless her cotton socks) poignantly reminding us all of the reasons why Amethyst exists and for whom—the women who come for support and help in a safe, nurturing environment. We were all very moved by what she said, including the griever, who finally said that she did not see herself pursuing the matter any further and decided to resign as she did not see a place for herself at the agency. I am exhausted but very relieved. I still think most of this could have been avoided if the outside union rep for the griever had made herself more aware of how we, at Amethyst, managed to conduct our negotiations for our collective agreement by consensus; instead, she seemed totally committed to an adversarial position right from the start, and by so doing, I think she did not serve her client well. I'm mad, as I was one of the strongest supporters of the union and have marvelled at the way we have all managed to work together. I only hope this doesn't destroy the trust we have built up over the years.

So, dearest Helen, this is the first time that I will hand you a letter instead of posting it. I'm afraid it wouldn't get to you before you leave if I snail-mailed it. Tired and all as I am, I am looking forward to the theatre tonight. With all this mess-up, I hardly remember my name, let alone what I am doing for the next few days. I postponed my singing lesson with Anna until tomorrow. I do have bits of shopping to do, as Aaron would not be impressed if I didn't have a gift for him on the 25[th]; neither would Helen or Chris. We are going to rent, or try to, all of the movies

[30] board member

that were made from Virginia Woolf's and E. M. Forster's novels—two years ago we rented eight videos of *The Jewel in the Crown*; it was terrific. Helen, this is very short, so I will probably hand you another one when we have lunch next week. Please don't forget to tell me the address in San Miguel.

With my love,
Oonagh xxx

Oonagh

January 7, 2002, 7 p.m.
In the kitchen, on my own!

Dearest Helen,

I can't believe how I have neglected you. Yes, I wanted to write but either didn't have the energy or just felt it was going to be a very boring letter. I seem to be very preoccupied these days with Amethyst stuff. Another major crisis has hit us. Sandi[31] is seriously ill in hospital. She had been in a coma for five days, and they are still not 100 percent sure what virus she has. She doesn't recognize anyone. Whatever it is has attacked her brain. Her friend Anna called her last Wednesday, January 2 and Sandi was talking gibberish. Anna rushed over to her apartment (Sandi lives on her own), took her to the Queensway Carleton, which promptly sent her to the General, where she is now. They have ruled out stroke, brain tumour and shingles on the brain (for two days that was the diagnosis). They changed it today, to what? We are waiting to hear. We are all in shock and exhausted.

To continue with the Amethyst saga. My life feels a bit unsteady at present. I can't, and no one else at Amethyst can,

[31] a long-time colleague from Amethyst

believe that I leave in six weeks. I have no regrets about my decision, but wish I could spend some quality time thinking about my farewell to clients.

Tuesday, January 8

As usual these days, I don't manage to do anything for very long. I got tired last night and ended up watching my favourite mystery program on TVO.

Chris was at a meeting—Fair Vote Canada, I think it's called. Maybe in our grandchildren's children's lifetime we might get proportional representation! The headline in the *Globe* this morning is "Canada opts for combat role"! What a wonderful society we have when the general feeling is one of disappointment that we are not sending our young people into war zones to kill an unknown enemy and end up in body bags themselves. It seems that in this war it is showing the world how important Canada is in the global police force. What an unfortunate lackey we are to the U.S. I love the idea of us being a peacekeeping nation. I think we do it well and don't have to prove ourselves to anyone, as we are known throughout the world for that.

As you can see, I am grumpy and totally fed up with the reasons given for starting wars, and I foam at the mouth when God is mentioned. More and more I become a confirmed atheist. Maybe on my deathbed, I'll need the comfort of an imaginary something, but until then godless I am, and godless I will remain. I give thanks to my father and my wishy-washy Catholic mother for counteracting the God stuff with solid arguments, and in Ireland in the '50s that was something—courage, foolishness, refusal to conform; whatever, I am very grateful. My Helen

thinks that bringing up children in an organized religion amounts to child abuse! What do you think?

January 11

Oh, Helen. What a terribly scattered and late, late letter this is. I was so confident that I would always manage every two weeks, come what may. Well, I haven't. I feel very discombobulated (Chris spelled this for me!). What with work and Sandi and my life and, and, and. My brain is in overdrive, so I feel either tired or wired! Saw Sandi yesterday. She has come out of the coma but can't walk and is speaking very slowly. They have now said it was an extreme case of viral meningio encephalitus, if you can believe them. She had three spinal taps, two MRIs and two CAT scans. She has her lovely laugh back and remembers most things now but is still very ill. I hope she can stay in a convalescent home before she goes home. She lives on her own, so somebody will have to stay with her. Her children, Stephanie and Ryan, are with her all the time. Ryan, who is twenty-six, sleeps on the floor beside her bed during the night. They have put their lives on hold to be with her night and day, as did her eighty-six-year-old mother. My concern is that there are too many visitors in and out, and nobody is saying anything.

I rarely visit people in hospital unless they are there for a long time. I think it is an intrusion, and we wouldn't charge into somebody's home the way we go, in droves, to hospital beds, thinking it's our right. So, Helen love, for the record, if I am ever in hospital, I will not expect you to come and visit. I have already told Chris and Helen. Of course if I phoned and asked you could you come, I hope you would; that's the control again. I just don't

want to feel like a sitting duck, having to make conversation when I don't want to, to people I don't want to see. God, I'm grumpy these days.

I think as I write this letter, the crisis at Amethyst is finally over. And I am so relieved that my colleagues are still in agreement with a unionized workplace. I know many feminists in the city were horrified when we unionized. I can understand why, and I am totally committed to unions. And I know how, historically, they have saved our lives, our jobs, our bread and butter, but it is very difficult to break down that mentality of adversarial confrontation. When I worked at Rideauwood many years ago, I was part of an EAP training program for postal workers. We, the staff of Rideauwood, would spend most of the time trying to get the management and the union membership to sit down, face each other and discuss problems together. At times, they nearly came to physical blows. So very different to what has been achieved at Amethyst over the years, and it all nearly collapsed in the last couple of months. When I say it's over, I mean the external part is—it will be a long time before the emotional scars heal. I hope, dearest Helen, this will be the last letter you have to read from me about this subject.

Saturday, January 12

Still haven't finished this. Foul means or fair, I will finish it today. I am sitting in my room, it's 9 a.m. I have decided to not shower, dress or eat breakfast until it's finished. Helen, my dear, I feel I'm going through a very strange time within myself. It's perhaps "normal" for a sixty-four-year-old woman, but for me it's disconcerting. I am finding I am not able to do six things at

once anymore. For example, it seems that I am putting so much thought and energy into Amethyst that I can't conjure up any enthusiasm to talk to friends, go to movies, etc. I forget to phone friends unless I see them or hear from them on a very regular basis. Chatting with Chris, playing Upwords, going for walks and my singing (I love it) is all I seem to manage. This is so very different for me, Helen. All these years I have managed to juggle all my roles—grandmother, friend, partner, counsellor, mother, actor, writer (recently), activist, and it seems that all of a sudden I can't do it. It is a major change, Helen, and a scary one for me. I weep as I write this. I haven't spoken about it to anyone other than Chris, who is very aware of these changes in me. I know that leaving Amethyst is so very right for me now, and I have a hope that things will sort themselves out in the months to come, and I will regain my ability (or some of it at least) to participate in activities I enjoy. Well, it's not activities, it's talking and listening to people except for the few close ones that's the problem. I love the idea of doing things with friends—bridge, singing, climbing mountains. I seem to have fewer and fewer close friends to sit and open my heart and soul to. You, Marilyn, Donna, and then I have to wonder if the relief of our letter writing and our closeness because of it, plus my burgeoning, changing friendship with my daughter, Helen, has helped change my needs in relationship to other friends. Methinks it has. So, as you can see, I am trying to work out what is happening to me. And to get some concrete answers to it all. And I hear you say, "Yes, Oonagh, good try"! I am amazed at what I write to you about. I feel so very confused, as you no doubt know, and yet I write to you about it all. This was not what I intended to write about this morning. I feel a great

sense of relief when I write. I know it does that for me, so why on earth don't I write more? If you have the answer to that, phone collect and tell me!

On to what I was going to write about. It looks as if we are going to St. Petersburg in September. Chris for three months, me, well, we'll see. I'll get an open ticket. Chris is thrilled, will be teaching a Canadian literature course and an English language one. We get an apartment free and enough rubles for food. I will certainly go for the first month. It's hard for me to imagine staying away from my home for three months, but the idea of living in a place for that long, not knowing the language, finding ways of communicating, etc. is intriguing. I think I should at least learn the Russian alphabet before I go, and the idea of having time to put a face to all the historical stuff is exciting. I'd see the Winter Palace. Wow! And Chris wants to do some research into his Jewish ancestors in Minsk. We would also probably visit Finland and go to Sweden. Karin will be there in September, and Niall thinks he will come and visit us in St. Petersburg. And yes, I would pop over to Dublin.

Oh, I am so pleased. I have managed to finish a letter to you. I will treat myself during the weekend to a phone call with you. It is so lovely to be able to imagine where you are, and El Jardin, where we will sit and watch the world go by, very soon.

With my love,
Oonagh xxx

P.S. Love to Gil.

Helen

January 13, 2002
San Miguel de Allende

Dear, dear, dear, Oonagh,

We've just come back from *Mrs. Dalloway*, a remarkable film directed by Marlene Gorris (Dutch, director of *Question of Silence* and *Antonia's Line*), with Vanessa Redgrave as Clarissa Dalloway. Don't have words to fully express my profound appreciation of the film and of Virginia Woolf. So full of personal and political, of personal as political, universal themes played out via individual lives and relationships. Clarissa's two-tiered conversations, internal and external. Her early refusal to marry Peter because he wanted to possess her completely and thus suffocate her. And her need for security—hence the boring politician husband Richard Dalloway. Her youthful friendship with Sally, their love, their hopes and dreams. The First World War and Septimus. The villainous shrinks, supposedly treating shell-shock, ignorant of the significance of war and suffering; losses, relationships (Septimus's friend blown up before his eyes); survivor guilt et al. Clarissa's endless parties as she struggles to bring momentary "cheer" into their world, her ongoing fear of failure, her second voice, her questions re past, present and future. I was in tears

toward the end. Partly in response to the film. And partly later on because I felt so desolate in San Miguel without a feminist soul-mate to talk with, rage with, explore meanings with, feel free to be *me* with, warts and all.

You phoned this morning, Oonagh, and we talked about this, among many, many other things. About you and Chris going to St. Petersburg in September, the joy of it, in different ways for both of you; of Sandi and her sudden illness and hospitalization; of your final gifts to Amethyst re PSAC[32] and CUPE; of having your retirement celebration in April (glad I'll be there) with all the women from the community invited and you *in control* of the event. I am grateful to have found a friend who needs to share, write, explode, weep and struggle. Who listens and who understands contradictions.

We went to brunch with our gang of six after your phone call. No tennis because of rain, none of us wanting to miss our post-tennis time together. It was, as usual, congenial, fun, stimulating.

With our friends here I feel that my feminism is accepted, perhaps even appealing in small, "reasonable" amounts. But the me who is angry and passionate and fed up with male dominance and wants to discuss *Mrs. Dalloway*, that me takes up little space.

I had lent Ellen *Savage Beauty* (about Edna St. V. Millay), which I loved. When I asked if she'd read it, at brunch, she had (reads fast), was fascinated by Millay's life but very disappointed in the book, felt it lacked literary art, tired of the author including every ounce of detail as in a thesis. There was no further discussion.

[32] Public Service Alliance of Canada

I remember it took me many years to begin to learn how to deal with and explore difference. I remember being particularly obnoxious during the Vietnam War when we lefties were all involved—demonstrating, housing and counselling war resisters, etc. I gave up on a few friends during that period because they seemed not to care much about our political interests.

With age and hindsight, I know my own behaviour was often pathetic and I needed to find out a lot more about exploring human connections rather than simplistically deploring them. And learning, if sometimes painfully. Which isn't an argument against ending friendships when they truly need to end.

Then there's Joan, an important San Miguel friend. Part of couple friends, as is Ellen. At brunch, Joan talked of her Boston book group—they're rereading all the classics by male authors, Dickens, et al. She hasn't come to any of the V.W. offerings, is sort of interested but not very. I'll talk to Joan when we're alone together; she's intelligent, open to exploring differences. But mostly we do things in couples, because that's the way it usually works in San Miguel. Which is different from my Ottawa life and has its own charms. In fact, I love this gang of six who play tennis and brunch together every Sunday morning, the guys and the gals.

I think of San Miguel as my second community.

Thanks for listening, Oonagh. I needed you tonight, more than you might imagine.

Now to the mundane pleasure of Upwords with Gil. Isn't life crazy! I think tangled relationships , the endless search for self and meaning, the personal as political—these are the themes of my existence. Have I repeated them over and over again since

childhood, without even knowing it? Is it like this for you, Oonagh? Bless Virginia Woolf for her genius and vision and courage. Bless Marlene Gorris for hers. While I stagger along in my muddled inner and outer life, bless the women who have helped us to understand and redefine our own lives. Bless Vanessa Redgrave who was a perfect Clarissa Dalloway. And bless you, Oonagh, for being my friend and writing partner and sidekick par excellence. I begin to sound as if I'm having a religious conversion! Good God, I'm really losing it now.

Why did they call women "hysterics" in the Victorian era? All that medical malpractice re hysteria. It was the men who were hysterical, with rage and temper tantrums and the abusive need to control and silence girls and women. Mr. Ramsay in *To the Lighthouse* exemplified all that. Cruelly and relentlessly and self-righteously and self-pityingly. Like V.W.'s father. The smug Ramsay whined and complained every time Caroline, his wife, left the house to do "good deeds" in the community. It was her only outlet, her only escape, her one contact with the outside world. But he begrudged her that because it meant less attention for him, less control over the kids whose noise diverted him from his attempts (futile) to reach "the summit" of his profession. What hysterics men were, are—why didn't, doesn't, the medical profession do something about their pathology? They're out of control with abuse, violence and wars. Let's invent a new DSM[33] for men, Oonagh.

Wish I'd studied English seriously as an undergraduate. It all seemed so boring back then—Chaucer, Beowulf, Milton. The

[33] Diagnostic and Statistical Manual of Mental Disorders

only authors I connected with then were the epic poets, the romantics who told stories of love and loss and beauty. My friend Betty and I used to read the poems to each other as we crammed for English exams in the middle of the night. Laughing and crying as we began to appreciate something called literature. Our prof was Minnie Gordon, one of the rare women faculty at Queen's in 1942. She was probably a remarkable scholar and pioneer, but I disliked her, and many of us taunted and ridiculed her at every opportunity. My loss, our loss, her loss. We needed to know her story, we needed to know her history, just as we needed to know why we held our own mothers to impossible standards and why we as girls and women were so insecure.

I think Christopher is lucky to have been an English prof. Shall I add this to my wish list of what might have been? Film too; I'd love to have been a film critic. *To the Lighthouse* and *Mrs. Dalloway* were unforgettable experiences of film.

January 15, 2002

I think there's something about bohemian communities, artistic communities, left-wing communities where the women *appear* to be more liberated, where equality *appears* to be taken for granted, but where the same old misogyny is operative. It's not that we heterosexual feminists are exempt from all this in our relationships. We are not, I am not. It's more that we struggle, consciously, with the men and the institutions that govern our lives, not just individually but collectively. We know we need other women in our lives to stay sane, to see and think clearly, without being subverted by our own colonized minds.

What on earth would I do in Ottawa, or anywhere else,

without my feminist friends and groups? Perhaps I've been ruined by these rich, personal/political connections so that I don't even know how to behave in the world at large. If I have given my daughters one gift, it is that sense of entitlement to their own separate, adult lives. They can't wait to come to Mexico beginning of March and will come on their own.

I'm happy to be here in San Miguel in all the ways I've written about before. And I feel lucky to have this winter break in an interesting, colourful and comfortable place. This community doesn't need me. I'm the outsider who will have to adapt, to fit in, to find my way.

Our CP is so near and dear to me, Oonagh. It provides a framework for my life these days. Everything, the good, the bad and the ugly, gets thrown in the hopper and there you are, at the other end, listening, reacting, knowing the *real* me better than most. Thank you for this rich friendship.

With much love,
Helen

Oonagh

Dearest Helen,

How about this for a thought? I am thinking (the thought is a seed at present) of walking all or some of the Camino Trail in Spain next year. It's a medieval pilgrimage walk to Santiago de Compostela. Maybe you have heard of it. A friend did it on his own in September, and when he talked about it a few days after returning I was fascinated and decided that one day I would do it. Anyway, I hadn't given it much more thought until Kieran, the friend, arrived yesterday with a copy of his journal. He has called it "a journal of my lifetime." I read it into the small hours of this morning, and by the time I came down for my coffee, I had decided I was definitely going somehow. I talked to Chris, who thought it was a great idea and asked, "When would we think of going?" I told him I wanted to go on my own, totally on my own, not with him, not in a group. He certainly expressed surprise but didn't hesitate to support my desire. Said that if I wanted him to meet me every four days somewhere on the way, he would do that. And, Helen, as this is only a seed of an idea, I could certainly change my mind about having someone else along. Whatever. I

do love the way he doesn't trample on my dreams, which allows me to explore possibilities and say yea or nay depending on my own needs and thoughts. My writing is a good example of this, as he has always encouraged me to "go forth and multiply my words"!

Anyway, I'm not thinking of going somewhere isolated. Thousands of people, young and old, do this walk twelve months of the year, so that there is always someone in sight or nearby. As I write this, it brings me back to my constant painful struggle, the collective vis-à-vis the individual. I think, as women, our natural (conditioning!) habitat is the community, and that individually and collectively we have a difficult time breaking free to do what we need to do on our own. I think that is why throughout history it's been the exceptions that are remembered as writers, painters, explorers, musicians; and I believe that men need to learn to become active within the collective, be that the family, the village, the boardroom, etc. I feel I am on a major rant here. I had a big argument with a professor when he kept saying the individualism of North American society meant every man for himself without thought for the community. He included me and all North American middle-class women in that statement. I asked him to explain, as I was not able to see myself outside of the family collective, and I tried to discuss with him how difficult it was for the majority of women to see themselves as separate individuals outside the collective, and how guilt-ridden we felt if we tried to step outside it. He didn't buy that, kept insinuating that I was denying my part in the whole individualism thing. What do you think of all this? I am beginning to think we are going to have to change this

into fiction, as we will both be outside of the collective if our friends and enemies see what we write about them. Oh, the freedom of it all!

Thursday, January 24

Received your wonderful, loving, newsy letter yesterday. Oh, the excitement of coming home, exhausted from Amethyst, to find you there. I barely said hello to Chris before I dashed upstairs, flung myself on the bed and buried myself in your words. I hope my letter wasn't a disappointment to you. I was so cranky, and rereading the beginning of this one, I continue to be. Oh, well. I loved being able to picture you in San Miguel; in your home there, on one of the three balconies; walking down the street (I hope all that weakness passed quickly, and has not returned); sitting in El Jardin. Are you still taking yoga? I think I might go to a few classes when I get there.

Saturday, January 26

Didn't get very far with writing on Thursday. What with my singing lesson, giving dinner to a friend of Chris's who was going to a concert with us (women composers' festival) and then off to choir practice.

Anyway, back to the concert. The music (chamber music) all by women composers. The first piece was by Louise Farrenc (1804–1875); I had never heard of her—what's new! It was exquisite. The other pieces didn't appeal to me, although Josephine loved the quintet by Amy Beach; I actually have heard of her. The festival was put on by the Ottawa Chamber Music Society, but the audience, compared with the crowds that go to hear their

summer concerts, filled only half the church. If it hadn't been for Chris, I probably wouldn't have gone either. He really is very attentive to women composers and women artists and over the years has given me a small, wonderful collection of books on women painters and CDs and tapes of music by women. I think this stems from his great love of women writers such as Virginia Woolf, Mrs. Gaskell, etc. And also his great love and knowledge of paintings and classical music in general; general meaning "male"! Imagine, we are in the twenty-first century, and that is still the case even though we are 51 percent of the population. Oh enough of that. It's not as if you don't know it all.

Sunday, January 27

What a disjointed letter this is. For someone who grumped about not wanting to yack with friends as much as I have done in the past, I managed to socialize a lot this week. Today I have nothing planned, and I love when I have nothing planned. Mind you, most of what I did last week was unplanned. It just happened, and I went along with it. That tells me I'm coming out of my slump. I was talking to my friend David Wiseman yesterday, and he too has been in a slump over the past month, what with David Pollock's death, and the world's chaos. Like me, he didn't want to see or talk to anyone. I feel consoled by our shared misery—mine for different reasons than his. Maybe not different, but as well as. Plus he's a dear friend.

Had my lunch with Christel. I am so very fond of her, and friends like her are very important additions to my life. In fact, they become more and more important as I get older and want to do things rather than soul search. One or two bosom friends are

enough, just as it was when I was a young girl. Although those friendships always seemed messy; usually a triangle, in and out of talking and not talking. Oh, so painful; a little bit of maturity helps. And the ability to allow ourselves the risk of being vulnerable. Writing that word reminds me of a neighbour I once had when Aaron was about eight. She told me I loved him too much and that I should protect myself, as Helen could easily move to the other end of the world, and what would I do then? I was shocked at her words. I told her that even if I knew that he was going to live elsewhere, even if I knew he wasn't going to talk to me ever again, I would still love him the way I loved him. And yes, I was open to heartbreak. In hindsight, I think I left myself open to a painful relationship with Helen, but not at the time—we both were so busy making sure that Aaron was loved and cared for.

For eighteen years, it seemed we put our relationship on hold. There were times we didn't want to talk to each other, but we did because of him—rightly or wrongly. I think we were both pretty amazing. I still think it would have been a lot easier if others had become involved and if Helen and I hadn't thought we were so alone. Not only with the physical stuff—she did most of that anyway—but with the nurturing. Chris eventually read stories and played table tennis with him. So, like many young boys, Aaron has not had a constant male role model. All his needs were met by women. I suppose that's no different from many families with men/fathers. Nancy Choderow said that each child needs five committed adults in his or her life.

Nelson Mandela was born into a small tribe, and all his mother and father's brothers and sisters were called Mother and

Father by the children, rather than Aunt and Uncle. So they never had love given and withheld by one or two parents, depending on behaviour. Something about communes that benefits parents and children. Adults are important but not important, and children the same. Is this all crazy talk? Am I blabbing on and on? And this talk about the glory of communes from a woman who craves aloneness and silence.

Dearest Helen, do finish *Savage Beauty* before I arrive as I would love to read it on holiday. The excerpts you sent whetted my appetite for more. If I finish the Iris Murdoch biography, I will bring it to you. I was somewhat concerned as it was written by a man, but I need not have been, as it's terrific. Peter Conrad and his partner, Jim, helped take care of her during her last few years of life; so Peter Conrad has written a wonderfully sensitive interesting bio. The movie *Iris*, just released, is based on John Bayley's book, and seems to be mostly about her illness. That pisses me off, as she was so much more than that. Maybe someone will make another movie.

I am going to finish here, as I don't want you to have to listen to my (at the moment) seemingly endless rantings. I'm sending you a copy of a short story that I wrote a few years ago. It has taken two years to edit. I pick at my stories and poetry as if they were scabs. Ain't that a disgusting image?

Hug to Gil.
Much love to your dear self,
Oonagh xxx

Helen
January 20, 2002

My dear Oonagh,

As you will undoubtedly have noticed, my writing deadline has gone awry. It was simply not possible for me to put pen to paper before this morning. Too many complications re settling in after a long, arduous flight (remind me to insist on an overnight stopover next year), Gil waiting for his MRI results ("pretty" positive; more on this later) and me getting a rotten cold with a bad cough. Add to the mix the seven-day Virginia Woolf festival in San Miguel—imagine!—which I am loving and appreciating in all kinds of ways, yet I am desperately missing my feminist sidekicks with whom I can be wild and unrestrained in my comments.

One of our friends thought it mighty strange that I was "seething" at times during the first presentation—short film and speaker. The speaker, and emcee throughout, was, a *male psychologist*! X! He was articulate, knowledgeable, interesting, but much too charming in describing a woman's life and art. He said all the right things, then added his bias re Virginia Woolf's pathology, mental illness, incest and marriage. No feminist

redefining, no alternative world view, no apparent consciousness of his inappropriateness in this key role. My friend Ellen whom I am very fond of, was there too. She's a feminist, but gentler, more accepting of men, less ideological. Inclined to be intellectual and literary rather than getting "too emotional, too biased" like me.

I needed you, Oonagh, needed my hot, opinionated, wild Irish friend who would listen, understand, agree and/or disagree without judgment.

Strange, I felt very much like my old friend Eva in this situation. She was known as "the bombshell" when we were both students at University of Toronto School of Social Work. An intense, explosive personality whom at times people didn't know what to do with. So Polish, so European, so Jewish (her "secret"), so Eva. I was an insecure, middle-class, mixed-up Ottawa kid, often embarrassed by her wilful, noisy explosions but drawn to her as a moth to a flame. She got into trouble the last few years of her life, in her mid- to late sixties, when her anger would spill over everywhere. I was the only one who wasn't afraid of it, knowing her so well with her need to love and be loved. She was certainly no feminist. We would have fought and argued about the male psychologist at the Virginia Woolf festival. Eva adored men, considered most of them her intellectual superiors. The sturdy foundation of our friendship always mattered more than our differences. Guess I can't have that sturdy foundation in SMA—how could I? This is only our fourth year here. I think you and I are in the process of building an enduring friendship, one that can allow for serious differences without crumbling. I hope so. Like Eva, I want to

love and be loved for the mad mix that goes to make up the essence of me. You, too, Oonagh?

I'm sitting in the sun on our first landing surrounded by greenery and gorgeous colourful blossoms—varying shades of pink, red, purple and green. Birds twittering, in trills. I can hear Anselmo, the condo gardener sweeping away at the pavement below. Otherwise quiet, peaceful, soothing.

Gil is doing well. He sleeps more and goes to the john more (probably side effects of hormones). He spends more time exercising at home. We played tennis on Sunday with our six-person gang, he continuously, me intermittently. Followed by our ritual brunch together. The hormones Gil is taking will impact on bone as well as prostate. They all say the best thing to do is to stay in Mexico, build up general health and have a good time. Which is what we both want to hear. Gil seems comfortable with the advice and glad to be here. Ruthie and Karen have been terrific—resourceful and caring, as always, working in tandem, phoning in tandem, conveying all the info clearly and effectively. We both feel lucky to have two such daughters in our lives. Gil feels well loved by them. As he is! I, of course, have to grab some of the credit by recalling that it was mainly I, their mother, who reared them in particular ways. Incorrigible, am I not, Oonagh?

I am conscious that you are back at Amethyst with all the worrisome complications around you as you begin to end. With clients and with yourself. How goes it? I assume it's not simple or straightforward; how could it be, given your long history there, the women who have come and gone and died, the recent mess, the battles won and lost? There were high hopes and

dreams for a feminist addiction service way back in 1979. And there was brave pioneering amid the "troubles" (not just Ireland); including your refusal to stay silent and conform. I hope I can be at your retirement celebration, or whatever you, Oonagh, are allowing them to do in your honour. My retirement was very important to me—the fight over it with Peter followed by his refusal, via phone, to have anything to do with the occasion. Then how Shirley and Colleen organized a women-only retirement dance for me at Carleton. Which was a smashing success— fun, laughter, dancing, the women's community there. And all the men's portraits on the walls—the men of "authority" who controlled Carleton—with eyes and mouths covered with masking tape. God, we were wild then. Deliciously wild!

Yesterday, enroute to the Virginia Woolf readings, I felt weak, faint and almost unable to walk. Just made it. Closest I've come to being one of the frail elderly. Fragile body. It was this cold and cough, in its final stages, having completely zapped me of all energy. I had visions of hospitals, of women tied into wheelchairs in chronic care institutions, limbs flailing, heads drooping, mouths drooling, making grotesque sounds. I need to die suddenly, unexpectedly, not as the prisoner of well- or not-so-well-intentioned staff who deem it their main task to keep their charges alive. I can only imagine the rage and despair that must curdle the souls within those helpless bodies.

I think Edna St. Vincent Millay did it right—didn't listen to advice of friends and relatives, lived on her own (with "help"), fell down the stairs, broke her neck and died.

I *loved* Nancy Milford's *Savage Beauty*, biography of Millay— the kids gave it to me before we left, I lugged all five hundred

pages of it, hard cover, to San Miguel. It was worth it; now going the rounds of my friends.

Going to get my hair cut, done. To be continued.

January 21, 2002

Am determined to get this letter to Border Crossings tomorrow morning when I go to yoga. Whether it's my usual length or not, whether I've written all I want to or not. Am enclosing a few xeroxed pages from *Savage Beauty* that jumped out at me. As did many others. Now reading *Clara Callan* by Richard Wright, letters between sisters and Clara's diary, reminds me of Margaret Laurence's *Fire Dwellers*, the internal and external conversation. Set in the 1930s with mood, language and way of life very familiar to me. One hilarious piece was sister Mae's description of getting involved with a Communist theatre group in New York City. Naïve, young Ontario kid, interested in acting and radio, grabs the opportunity without any awareness of political implications. I read it aloud to Gil, in hysterics with laughter and almost unable to control my reading. Guess it touched nerve endings re some of my own early political encounters.

Surprised I'm reading a male author? I am, sort of. It was Karen who insisted the book was for me regardless of gender. She was right. Friend Ellen here is going to lend me one of Primo Levi's books; have never read him, always wanted to. My feminist book group at home mostly keeps me on the straight and narrow as to choice of reading. Which is where mostly I want to be.

Four women read from Virginia Woolf's novels yesterday at the festival. One reading, from *Mrs. Dalloway*, was simply superb. I was stunned by the reader's artistry. Told her so after. I

understood *Mrs. Dalloway* as never before, simply because the reader transported me, sensitively and articulately, into the place and mood and meaning of the work. Someone else read from *The Waves*, which also tantalized me.

I got such a late start at carving out what I now deem to be an interesting life. I'd love to have taken a serious crack, with training of some kind, at doing dramatic readings, at writing, yoga, singing and performing in some way. *Savage Beauty* tells of Millay as poet and performer, the latter an important part of her life. God, such unfulfilled desires I have and so little time.

Gil thinks we should organize a Virginia Woolf festival in Ottawa—simply transplant the formula. He's always dreaming up projects for me, as if I had energy to burn. He includes you in this one. Don't think I'd choose Virginia Woolf—don't know her work in depth—but lots of other possibilities. Might be something my feminist envisioning group might do. No wonder women and women's movements and feminism go underground for fifty year periods. The stresses and strains of trying to budge the status quo, hold on to the changes in the face of overwhelming backlash and survive the pressures of an individual woman's life—all of this and more often grind us into grease spots.

To the Virginia Woolf festival again today—to see the film *To the Lighthouse*. Tomorrow, Saturday, will be quiet—just yoga, reading and Upwords. And Esperanza's enchiladas, which she made for us today. I'm loving the food here, as always, but have to watch that I don't get carried away so that my digestive system stops functioning.

This is it, Oonagh! End of letter. I'll try to make up for the gap by writing sooner next time. Not keeping a journal in San Miguel

this year; letters will be replacement. Can't wait till you and Chris come to San Miguel.

I'm so glad our lives are all tangled up together. Can't imagine how I ever made sense of mine without our letters. You are a much beloved friend.

Love to Chris and mutual friends. Await your letter impatiently.

Helen

Oonagh

Tuesday, February 5, 2002, Not Spring!

Dearest Helen,

February 1 is the first day of spring in Ireland—crocuses, bluebells and daffodils in the woods and along the roadways. When I went to Dublin on my mountain-climbing trip four years ago, the road from the airport into the city had thousands and thousands of daffodils on either side and down the centre; talk about the yellow brick road and rainbows! Ottawa today is a far cry from that memory as it is snowing heavily and -28° (with no wind chill). I shouldn't grumble, as up until two days ago, I was walking all over the place. It sure makes a difference having the winter start so late, added to the fact that we arrive in San Miguel in ten days' time, so that when we get back in early March, the end is in sight.

I was going to drive to Mountain Equipment Co-op, but decided to write to you instead. I work this evening, and a number of my clients have asked to be in my group (there are four groups running on Tuesday evenings). Even some of my colleagues' clients have asked to be there; it makes me feel appreciated and loved. I have spent the last couple of weeks

organizing my files (the bane of my life at the best of times), trying to match up the women I was seeing to a counsellor they could work with. And as you know, we are so short-staffed that it is difficult to accommodate everyone. I am a strong believer in the power and support of groups, so I am urging the women to make full use of them. The motto here is Don't do as I do, do as I say, as I would never have opened my feelings and thoughts in a group when I was going through depression. It was hard enough opening up to one other person. Mind you, I did always have one friend that I confided in when I was going through painful times.

February 11, 12 noon

Dearest Helen, this is the first and only time I have taken time at work to write a personal letter. My motto has been When at work, work, and when at home, do all the other stuff. Decided to write to you today as I am totally overwhelmed with the work ahead but do so want to write to you so that you can receive this when I am in San Miguel. Saturday seems such a long way off. I am trying to take one hour at a time. Last night I could have written to you, but I spent about an hour trying to decide what to wear at Helen's "call to the bar" on Thursday. Can you believe that? I became somewhat frantic, so by the time I had tried on practically everything I own, returned to what I had decided to wear in the first place a week ago! And my bedroom was a disaster area, and my relationship with Chris had deteriorated into a yelling match; sigh, sigh, sigh. So this week, I leave Amethyst (4 p.m. Wednesday). It's Chris's birthday, so I usually try to do something special. I am thinking of taking him out to breakfast before coming in to work. That's special, eh?

I have just finished a rough draft of a letter to one of our relief counsellors. The reason? Well, last Tuesday, five minutes before we went into group, she said, in response to my leaving, that she wouldn't work at Amethyst as it was a very destructive place, very conservative and all the staff were fearful, and she worried about the clients! I was not able to respond but felt very upset at what she had said. I decided to write to her, to suggest she go to staff and board with her concerns and (more important) to clarify my own feelings about Amethyst. You know yourself, Helen, how critical I have been over the years; nevertheless, if I was to live my life over again, I would be working at Amethyst for twenty-one years or more.

February 12

I have cleared out my office. I find it really strange, as none of the old crowd is here and the few staff who are here are so busy and stressed out that they haven't time to sit and talk about my leaving. Erin and Marguerite don't believe I'm going! This morning before I came to work I packed my bag for Mexico, so I feel a little less stressed. I bought Chris two books and a very nice fleece vest for his birthday and wrapped them up. God, ain't I organized! And Edwin and I have bought a state-of-the-art laptop computer for Helen's graduation on Thursday.

Sunday, February 17

San Miguel, relaxed after a great sleep, a lovely breakfast and the sun is trying to shine. This garden is just lovely and as it's a little cool I am here on my own. When we went into breakfast, there was a singer with a guitar. Not a great voice, and rather

loud, but we still managed to speak to two couples. For someone who loves the silence of early morning coffee with Chris, I sure yacked a lot this morning. One couple from Michigan, both teachers, and she, Joanne, teaches writing to handicapped young adults. When we went to introduce ourselves, she turned to Chris and said, "We know you are Christopher Levenson"! They had seen many posters. Unfortunately, they leave on Tuesday.

Now back to our heavenly meeting in the El Jardin. I think I might have appeared somewhat spacey, did I? It always seems to take me a day or two to recover from travelling, and I think it will take me weeks to recover from the hectic week I had. Helen, you look so well, and so relaxed, and as always were so interested in my life. I feel so very cared for by you, and so welcomed by both you and Gil. And I was charmed by your friends, Joan and Jeffrey. What's marvellous about our neighbours from the U.S. is that those I have met are great at asking questions, and finding out, at least on the surface, who you are, unlike many Canadians, who find it difficult to ask the questions. I once asked someone why Canadians didn't ask questions, and she replied that it was rude! I then said that I felt that it was indifference. She was shocked when I said that. Do you think maybe that's one of the cultural differences between Canadians and Americans? Can you imagine all the assumptions people make when they don't ask questions?

I had dreams all night about Amethyst and my children, in particular Paul and Rachel. In the past, my dreams have always helped me sort out my feelings, and more and more I realize that my "role" as counsellor has been one of the most positive roles in my life—that and my grandmothering of Aaron, the two roles

that I have no regrets about. Both I did well. So, dearest, that's where the grieving is going to come from—my loss of a very important role. I have to tell you, I have moved back inside our room, as too many people are about, and as I look out of the window, there is a group of people talking to Chris about his poetry and the reading. He is in his element; I'm in mine too, lying on the bed writing!

Tuesday, February 19

The morning after our great evening together with Joan and Jeffrey. They are a very easy couple to converse with, and argue with too! Lawyers are good at that, and I like the way they both hold on to their views, even in the face of strong opposition. I can understand why you and Gil like them so much.

Shit. The guy who sings at breakfast every morning is now out on the veranda belting out Spanish "musik" and I have now lost my train of thought, and it was so nice out here writing to you, listening to the birds and the quiet. I would love to tell him to shut up, but I don't know the Spanish for shut up, and anyway I don't think it would be a good idea, as he is the owner's father. He has a good voice, but for breakfast and early morning I could do without it, and, looking at the faces at breakfast, I think everyone else feels the same.

Fifteen minutes have passed by since I wrote this. I finally stormed into our room, glaring at him. He got the message, as he has disappeared. Where was I? Yes, Joan. I like the way she speaks, as if her emotions and her intellect are working together—a thoughtfulness. Do you see her on her own, I wonder? I have met a number of male lawyers like Jeffrey,

argumentative and charming, and I always feel I have nothing in common with them, so don't pay much attention; how dismissive can I get. Debating is not what I'm about.

By the way, Chris thinks that the topic of poetry produces the same reaction as the topic of feminism. People get uncomfortable and then decide to tell jokes and ease the seriousness of a discussion. Actually, I suggested that to Chris, and he agreed. It's too good a comparison to give him the credit.

I could have spent the evening talking about hospital visits. Can't remember at all what I wrote to you before, but I know it was in relation to Sandi and my own feelings about having my privacy respected if I ever went into hospital. It's also reacting to the expectation that if I know someone is in hospital, I should go and visit, even if they are casual acquaintances. I can't or won't do that. I want my dearest friends and my family to know that they are important and not just anyone; and that what I do for them and with them is because I love them and they are so important to me. Having said that, I think the whole idea of women's caregiving role underlies all of it. The expectations that both women and men have, that the women, be they daughters, wives, friends, mothers, will take care of them in sickness and in health; and even the feminist movement hasn't dealt with that in any depth. Maybe it can't be dealt with very easily, but deal with it we have to, or women will continue to end their lives feeling resentful and full of rage and doing things out of duty rather than because they want to.

My mother went away, and took care of older people until they died. She was innately a great caregiver—loving, humorous. But when she reached the age of seventy-five she found a small

flat in Cambridge and holed up there, taking care of herself, occasionally seeing a few people when she felt the need, but she certainly gave up on caregiving for others; she was totally worn out.

Dearest Helen, this must sound extremely garbled. I find it difficult to write when I feel so deeply about something. I do so believe in community and all of us caring for each other, spreading it around so that no one feels overwhelmed, but that does not happen, and so the caring is left to the already overworked and tired women. What to do?

It's time to go to the El Jardin to meet with you and while away the hours with you.

My love as always, dearest friend,
Oonagh xxx

Helen

My dear Oonagh,

No blue sky, no hot sun, puddles left over from heavy rain last night, damp/chilly house. I've got the one little heater on in the living room and am wearing layers to keep warm. There were two days like this in January and now two in February. It promises to be warm tomorrow, and hopefully the weather will be gorgeous again by the time you and Christopher arrive Friday night. Gil can't figure out why I'm writing to you today, given your imminent arrival. But for me, one thing has little to do with the other. And after not being in a writerly mood for a while, today I want/need to talk with you on paper.

Your delicious letter arrived with clippings and short story. I so love getting mail here and always, wherever, your mail. There were all kinds of clicks for me in what you wrote about, so I may do more responding than usual. I appreciated what you said about Chris "not trampling on your dreams" (beautifully expressed). So, so important. My view of most women's lives is that our dreams do get trampled on, very early and often cruelly. I always remember a workshop I did with older women years

193

ago, when I asked participants to recall their hopes and dreams at age eighteen. One woman in particular, there with her daughter, remembered her fun-loving, optimistic personality, how she loved dancing, being with people. That all changed with marriage and she had gradually lost her sparkle and her "life."

I read that part of your letter to Gil (I hope you don't mind), plus your comments re PSAC (Public Service Alliance of Canada) and CUPE. He reminded me that we come to San Miguel each winter because this is what I in particular need and want. He likes it too but often would prefer to travel to new places. I guess I was connecting re "wilder" dreams. The only one I can think of at the moment is buying a small scooter (motorized) and chasing around Ottawa on it. I, of course, could do just that, but it's the encouragement I need to make it okay and to let it happen. I also liked C's offer to meet you every four days on the Camino Trail—takes imagination to dream up that kind of possibility!

It's damn important to have dreams in the first place, all through life. So bully for you, Oonagh, re the Camino Trail, whichever way it suits your fancy. It wouldn't be my dream, but that's the thing about dreams. Maybe the point is being able to hear other women's wonderful imaginings without projecting one's own value system or one's own fears. I love the fact that Rachel is traipsing around Nepal, Thailand all on her own, that none of us tried to persuade her otherwise.

Your clipping about *The Book of Eve* being made into a film with Claire Bloom—that story is for sure about taking one last stab at the possibilities, the dreams. Like your mother! I loved the book and loved Constance Beresford Howe's writing—she sort of reminds me of Ethel Wilson (*Mrs. Golightly and Other Stories*). I once heard C.

B. Howe speak. She talked about the hard work in every sentence written (it all read so effortlessly) and about the book not being a call to arms for feminists (many of us took it that way).

It's now 4:30 a.m.; can't sleep, went to bed early. And also we've got too much social stuff in the next few days, including too many meals out in restaurants. I get edgy when this happens. I want to see people, like them, don't want to be ignored or left out, but I need that fragile balance between doing and being, between silence/aloneness and socializing and friendship. I don't think I'll ever get it right, partly because it can't be entirely within my control.

We went to a PEN (writers) lecture last night by the daughter of Holocaust survivors. She's written a novel, some poetry, has just retired from teaching creative writing in California. Bought a house in San Miguel, plans to write full time. Themes of grief, loss, hope, healing and the dangers of silence and family secrets. Very articulate, solid on family dynamics, interesting.

One of the women in the audience talked about how the father is the hero of the novel. The author deftly responded by speaking of both parents. The woman's husband is an active member of the Jewish community in SMA. He "asked" a question, the kind of question that lets you know, with each word uttered, that he is "scholarly" and has very important things to say. I, as ever, react negatively to know-it-all men.

I was intrigued by what you wrote re individuals and community, the differing needs! I had just finished reading the biography of Véra Nabokov titled *Véra*. I knew nothing about her or husband Vladimir, except that he had written *Lolita*.

She's a visceral anti-Communist, a believer in the supremacy of the individual, a dedicated wife who considered her husband a genius, did all the work in all spheres to enable him to write (even his personal and professional correspondence). Highly opinionated, unafraid of social disapproval, talented, rendered herself mostly invisible by sharing little of her life (other than opinions and being Jewish). Partly, she reminded me of Eva, who considered her Walter a genius, a superior intellect and who was highly opinionated. But she, Eva, had a life and work of her own and close women friends.

I think I veer to the community side of the equation. I need more of a sense of community in my life, a rootedness, a place where I easily and comfortably belong. Which is partly why feminism and the women's movement made such an impact. It's about injustice and inequality, but it's also about belonging. I was always a misfit in conventional communities, needed more of a sense of purpose and meaning beyond my own existence. I'm still into some of the "shoulds" around loyalty and obligation. My sense of you, Oonagh, is that you veer toward the other side of the equation, with more emphasis on individual freedom of action and refusing conventional expectations.

I have to tell you, dear soul mate, referring to an earlier letter, that being visited in hospital is way high up on my list of expectations. Without asking! Now how are we going to work that one out, given your conviction re not invading and what people need when hospitalized. I hate having to ask for what I need when I'm vulnerable or fragile. I want people close to me to figure it out or ask me. This is an area where Ruthie and I have had our struggles and push each other's buttons.

To be continued—I need some sleep before getting up for yoga. I love my yoga class, hope you will come with me when you arrive in SMA. Can't wait to see you, Oonagh. It's been a long stretch without you to brighten up my life.

February 13, 2002

The weather has cleared, sun has emerged, our patio awaits you. Also some of our friends and acquaintances. I've warned them that you, Oonagh, are not about to let me or anyone else organize you, that you guard your freedom of movement, your independence, at all times. So whether they think you're a radical, a recluse or a renegade, who cares. The only arrangement planned, as per our agreement, is Monday evening dinner with Joan and Jeffrey at their house. And of course Christopher's poetry reading on February 20. Gil began to post and distribute the flyer he has put together with Christopher's picture prominently displayed. There will also be a press release in *Attencion*, which comes out the Sunday before the twentieth. Gil, as Ruthie says, is just an impresario at heart. We're hoping for a good turnout!

Tomorrow night, we go to a Valentine's party at Elaine and Bob's. Elaine likes program, asks people to bring prose/poetry to read. Worked pretty well last year, though there are always dissenters in the crowd. She's asked me to emcee it this year, which I've agreed to do, with her. I'll use my favourite poem *"Be Kind, My Love"* which was written by Elaine's first husband. You and Chris would probably enjoy the readings, but the crowd of strangers would definitely not be your cup of tea. I was like a stray waif at last year's party until the program got under way.

Since the *Globe*'s "Facts and Arguments" hasn't grabbed my

story re our glorious CP I have another topic in mind—the Levine foursome ritual of having an annual holiday together. Sounds boring (as an article) but any parent I talk to loves the idea. They see it as impossible with their adult children who have families. Being with their kids only is not allowed, adult children come in family packages. The institutions of marriage and family dictate that primary bonds with spouse and kids predominate. Those bonds are supposed to be nurtured by older parents. I would never have gone away with my parents and siblings—the idea would have been preposterous. I went "home" to visit with kids, but that was a whole different kettle of fish. It could be fun to look at the ingredients required to make an "early family" holiday even a possibility. I'm intrigued with the topic.

I have a great confession to make, Oonagh: I love having a "maid." For our two months in San Miguel, Esperanza works about four hours a day, five days a week. It's such a luxury having everything, but everything, organized for us each day. Sadly, we really can't get to know her because we're so hopeless with Spanish. Things seem to work out comfortably for the three of us.

But one never knows what it's like to be in the worker's shoes. There has to be plenty of resentment re the rich North Americans and the poor Mexicans. The contrasts are huge. Nevertheless we live in our own little cocoon pretty comfortably, despite the larger reality. Not so different at home—variations on the same theme.

End of letter. End of correspondence from Mexico. The time has flown and we'll be home in a few weeks. And we're going to see you in San Miguel this coming weekend. How wonderful! I can hardly believe that we've found these remarkable ways to be connected.

Gil and I are about to play Upwords—we're sharpening our claws for the coming tournament with you and Chris.

<div align="center">

Lots and lots of love,
Helen

</div>

P.S. I was very sad about Princess Margaret's death. Had watched Masterpiece Theater's *Elizabeth and Bertie* (excellent) and also a documentary on Elizabeth II. Do you know that I've been smitten with curiosity and fascination with the royals since childhood—me and my mother. Like her, I gobble up all the media stuff about them. No one, but no one I know gives a damn, including my kids. When I was the shabbiest and most plainly dressed young woman my mother ever knew, she would say to me, she who was fastidiously dressed and groomed, "I would go with you like that"—meaning my clothes—"to Buckingham Palace." Big compliment and she meant it. My father would give me money to go out and buy decent clothes!

Memories, memories. I revel in them.

Oonagh

Tuesday, March 5, 2002
2:30 p.m., in the kitchen

Dearest Helen,

Silence reigns! Chris is out, and I'm in my favourite writing room, having a cup of tea and writing to you. I am so delighted to be home. I have slept well the last two nights, although I dream about Amethyst a lot. The second phone call I had on Sunday was from a woman whom I had seen twenty years ago. She heard I had retired and wanted to say hello and to let me know how important I had been to her during her time at the agency. She said she used to try to get to group early so that she could sit beside me! Like Canada, Amethyst is much a part of me. What a very different person I would be today if I hadn't had the wonder of all those marvellous women. They got into my bloodstream, Helen, set me up for whatever the future might bring.

March 7

In the kitchen again, for a brief time only, as Chris will be back soon. He also loves writing here. Helen, what a grand time we had with you and Gil in Mexico City. I loved it. I loved watching your delight and excitement at being there, your wonderful,

thoughtful response to the art exhibition. Your, oh, so charming delight in the behaviour of that young boy who sat with us; your pleasure at the hordes of people, the jacaranda trees, as if you saw them for the very first time; the buildings, the hotel, everything. It was one of the highlights of our visit to Mexico City. It is usually so hard for me to be with anyone for that length of time without a break, but that day, with both of you, it was just perfect in every way. I can't recall a time when I felt so relaxed over so many hours in the company of friends, walking, taxiing, talking, laughing, eating. Well, actually mountain climbing with others has the same effect. I think it's the movement, not sitting for hours, and the chatting in an offhand and casual manner. Does that make sense? More about this later. God, Helen, I can be extremely difficult at times; as if you didn't know! I think it gets back to "doing" things with friends—playing bridge, tennis, walking, whatever. I love my lunches with close friends, but the intensity I can take for only a few hours at a time, and then I need to move, to be with myself.

Friday, March 8

Thinking of you today. Mind you, I think of you most days and chat to you in my head about all sorts of things. Paul Knox wrote a good column in the *Globe* this morning about International Women's Day. I liked the last paragraph in particular; will keep it for you. I am again in the kitchen, the house to myself—the peace of it all! Aside from my singing yesterday, I have pottered about all week without any commitments to anyone or anything. It has been pure bliss. Two days in a row I didn't get dressed until 2 p.m. I now have time to dream and

catch up with my thinking without the rush. No matter how busy I've been in the past, I always tried to leave time for the unexpected to happen. Even if that was only an hour a day, but at times recently that has been hard to do. As you are no doubt aware, dearest friend, I am very conscious of time—being on time, balancing time. I think I would have done well in a monastery life. Pray a little, garden a little, eat a little, talk a little, etc. Friends have expressed exasperation with me over the years when I have refused to allow our lunch get-togethers to go over two hours.

At work, I always started groups on time and finished on time, even though I don't wear a watch. Part of it is physical; I can't sit for hours. My body aches, and I become so conscious of my physical discomfort that it takes over my concentration. The other part is intellectual and emotional. I have tried to work out over the years why I can't cope with long stretches of time with people, even close friends. And I have come to the realization that when I am with someone, for example having lunch, I am totally and completely with that person intellectually, spiritually, emotionally. So much so that my energy becomes depleted, and I need to withdraw into myself. There have been times at work when I would come out of a group or individual session not remembering my name or where I was. Losing myself in the moment, which is great. However I also think it's hard for others to understand. So, dearest one, the fact that your visit to Mexico City was so fantastic is and was awesome, to use the expression of the young!

Methinks it also has something to do with our letter writing, and allowing you to see me and feeling accepted with all my

contradictions and just relaxing into your friendship. The visit we had with you and Gil in San Miguel on the Sunday after we arrived was the same; a great easiness about it, and then there was our own private lunch on the Tuesday, and the confiding.

I loved meeting your friends there, Helen. And they made us feel so welcome and so very special. Chris and I felt that their generosity toward us both reflected your love for us, Helen, and their love for you and Gil. When Joan said that she was so relieved to know that you had a friend like me in Ottawa, I too am so delighted to know that you have such loving, caring friends in San Miguel. But, Helen, you have the most wonderful friends all over the place. If I were to write your epitaph, I would say, "Here lies a woman who knew what friendship with women was all about; she gave and received in a spirit of generosity, humour, delight, interest and intelligence." Well, love, that's just off the top of my head; imagine what I could do with this with more thought! I think I'm good at this sort of thing. Marilyn has informed all her family that I am to be her eulogist when she dies. That is, if she dies before me. I do hope, Helen, that you have no regrets in your role of friend. I should have mentioned intense, honest and risk-taking; even if it means the end of a friendship, Helen. And you have it in spades, hearts, diamonds, clubs, and trumps!

Sunday, March 10

You'll be back today, and I haven't finished this letter. Well, I'm going to deliver it, finished or not. I have just read an article about Zimbabwe and, yes, I can understand why the African states decided not to put sanctions on it, why they didn't go

along with the "white" commonwealth countries; but I do have problems with "blind loyalty" for the sake of sticking together, and I think there will now be civil war. So, you say, join the rest of the world. Have you ever read Charlotte Bunch? I wrote a paper once on Irishwomen and native women and quoted her. She said that

> From a feminist perspective, nationalism is the ultimate expression of the patriarchal dynamic of domination. On one hand, groups battle for control over geographic territory; on the other hand, nationalism symbolizes the struggle of oppressed peoples against the takeover by other nations, thus seeking to be global. Feminists have to find ways of transcending atriarchal nationalism without demanding sameness, and preserve a means of identity that is not based on dominance.[34]

Somewhat utopian, eh?

I feel myself becoming more and more detached from the world of political misinformation and corruption. So I contradict myself, having just read the article on Mugabe. He took his country into independence with grace and integrity. What the fuck happened? I think he has something wrong with his brain now, and is surrounded by thugs. Detached, eh?

And then there is Ireland—Republic of Ireland, that is. They have had yet another referendum on abortion. The no side of the existing law won by 2 percent—51 percent to 49 percent. If the yes side had won, women who had had abortions could have got up to twelve years in prison if they

[34] *Passionate Politics*, Charlotte Bunch (New York: St. Martin's Press), 1987

were found out. The anti-abortionists wanted the law tightened, and that includes the present government! Only 45 percent voted, and thank God the majority of votes came from Dublin and its surroundings. Priests in the small towns still have enormous power. Was it Marx who said, "Religion is the opium of the people"? True, true, true. Thank whatever that I had an atheist father and a wishy-washy Catholic mother who had little or no time for the Church hierarchy. Ireland is constitutionally a secular state; can you believe it!

As a child I hated sticking out like a sore thumb, but, oh, am I so glad I (we) did. Dearest Helen, I can't believe that I wrote, just one page ago that I was becoming more detached. I guess I should have written "I would like to become more detached"!

Now back to friendship, your friendships. To prove everything I said about you and friendships, the e-mails I have received from Susan Zettel confirm it all. The time she took; the interest she is taking in our project; the belief she has that we will and can do it. Oh, Helen, to see this down on paper from someone outside ourselves is scary and marvellous at the same time.

I have enclosed all the e-mails from her. It seems to me that we are doing it for not only ourselves but also our friends (those who are not going to sue us, that is!), our families (those members who won't disown us, that is) and our enemies; at least we can be sure of their reactions! I do love the way our friends are not at all threatened by our writing. That's love, Helen, unconditional.

I want you to get this today so I'm going to finish here. I wanted to respond to your "family away." I just can't imagine my

kids and I doing that for more than a brief lunch. I can't cope with family get-togethers at any time. One-on-one, sister, brother, son, daughter, mother, father, even grandchildren. Aaron and I have a grand time when we go out together. Put Helen and Chris into it and yuck, although that's not quite true: when Helen, Aaron and I went to visit my ma many years ago, it was terrific. I could imagine going away with each of them one-on-one and doing different things with each of them on my own. Control you say! Right!

> Thrilled to pieces you are home.
> My love, to you, dearest friend,
> *Oonagh* xxx

Had some articles for you to read; can't find them now. One of the delights of coming home was reading the *Guardian Weekly*. The news is so different from what we get here—at least, the perspective is. Not only from the *Guardian* but from *Le Monde* and the *Washington Post*.

Oonagh
Monday, March 18, 2002

My dear Helen,

I am delightfully housebound. This is one of these days when I love to have appointments cancelled because of the weather— so here I am, in my room, writing to you. I was in the kitchen, but Chris is pounding away on his manual typewriter in his study, and I could hear every "pound" in the kitchen. I told him last week that I am going to buy a tape of Leroy Anderson's "The Typewriter" and play it at his memorial service. He is now trying to find ways of having my memorial first!

So now on to other things. Guess what I have discovered? A feminist publisher in Toronto—how come I didn't know of them? Anyway, I found their website (I hope you are impressed) and I think we should submit our letters to them. Maybe two each, plus a brief description of what we are about. It takes them four months to process and read manuscripts. What do you think? I got sort of excited this morning when I reread my first letter to you, and aside from one sentence, I'd leave it as it was written. There were no nasty comments about friends and family. On top of getting excited about our letters, I decided to send them a short

story which I wrote a few years ago about a young boy with a lesbian mother. I think it might have potential as a novel for young adults, or maybe connecting short stories. Anyway I'll post it today and see what happens. So there you are, dear friend, having woken up feeling very discombobulated, I have now changed my outlook, at least for today. I am definitely a behaviourist.

Tuesday, March 26

A whole week has gone by and I haven't written one word to you. I wish, oh, how I wish I could keep a little tape recorder close to my head, so that I could record all the marvellous inner conversations I have with you each day. Over the week I have been dealing with a mini-crisis in the family, and when not dealing with it, I have been recovering from having to even think about it and them! Your loving, thoughtful phone call the other day meant so much, Helen—the fact that there was someone who remembered what was going on in my life. So, my dear friend, I am in the third week of my retirement from Amethyst. The reality is finally settling in—up until a few days ago, I felt I was on holidays. When I explore, deep down, my decision to leave, I know without a doubt it was the right decision and the right timing. I am slowly realizing that it not only took up a lot of my external thinking and energy, but was also there when I wasn't consciously thinking about it. The gap that is left in me is huge, giving me an enormous sense of relief and release on one hand, and *what on earth is going to take its place?* on the other hand. I have never been good at filling my life with "make-do projects." My work outside of my home has, for the most part, been a vocation, which meant I would have done it whether I got paid

or not—that is, if I could have afforded to not get paid. I think I was very lucky when I came to Canada that I managed to find work that I was totally committed to and passionately believed in, whether that was with women, handicapped children, addictions, or my short, magical role as a Unitarian chaplain. I would love to think that writing was going to be a major part of my future—and I do think it is. However, I am an activist and I just can't see that side of me disappear overnight, but I am not going to jump into anything fast. I intend to do those activities I already do more slowly and thoughtfully, allowing the process to happen. Sounds good on paper!

I am realizing more and more that the events of September 11 and its aftermath have affected me deeply, in much the same way as the Cuban crisis did. Although I skim over the newspapers (with the exception of the *Guardian Weekly*, which I read from cover to cover) and barely listen to or look at the news, I am so aware and frightened of how fragile our world is, and how trigger-happy the U.S. is with their weapons of mass destruction. No doubt those earthquakes in Afghanistan are the direct results of the U.S. bombing in those wonderful barren mountains. The only comfort I have at present is that during the Cuban crisis, I thought the world was going to end, and it didn't—at least for us in the West! For many years my negative thoughts about the U.S have lain dormant—or at least way down my list of what to worry about. Even after the Gulf war, I managed to put my feelings on one side. Now the U.S. is all back in spades again. I trust them less and less, so this is when I wished I lived some-where in Europe. I spent a lot of time in therapy trying to deal with my global feelings, and in the end I managed to get them

into some sort of perspective (for me anyway!) and focus on those issues that I could change (including myself). Hopefully the same thing is going to happen again, so that I can get rid of the bile in my throat whenever I hear or see mention of what the U.S. government is saying or doing or planning. As a friend, I don't trust them, and as an enemy I don't trust them. That's a pretty major statement eh? What enormous power we, the rest of the world, allow them.

I am sure this page will be one of your least favourite to read. You have probably heard it all before from Gil. Enough of all this.

Wednesday, 8 a.m.

As usual, something took me away from you, and then I was supposed to have a singing lesson and last night we went to the NAC[35] and saw Robert Lapage's magnificent play, *The Dark Side of the Moon*. I think he is the best French/English language director/playwright in the world today! How about that for praise? I thought last night's play was superb—fifteen minutes too long— but amazing, funny , sad, informative, clever and very gimmicky in that he uses technology, such as lighting, video and puppets. He wrote this particular play after his mother died. The basic story is about his younger brother and himself cleaning out their mother's apartment after her funeral. I haven't the words to do it justice. It was theatre at its most magic. At the end the audience got up as one and paid homage to him.

So, dear friend, I have not written about the stuff around family. It will have to wait for another letter or maybe never get

[35] National Arts Centre

written at all. I am having lunch with Joan Wilcox and dinner with Donna tonight. I swore I wouldn't make more than one commitment a day. That lasted all of three days! I am writing this lying on my tummy on the floor in the bedroom. Just for this brief moment I feel like a young girl again. I used to lie in the field outside of our home in Shankill and read and write and dream—and plan my get-away! Are you going to see the play in GCTC[36]?

<div align="center">

Much love,
Oonagh xxx

</div>

P.S. Chris has just told me that I put the oatmeal in the fridge this morning. The full moon is tomorrow; maybe that's what made me do it. When in doubt, blame the elements or the U.S!

[36] Great Canadian Theatre Centre

Helen
Thursday, March 28, 2002, end of Passover

My dear Oonagh,

I have not abandoned our beloved CP, just gotten stuck for a little while en route from San Miguel, Mexico City and Rio Yucatán. Good thing we're meeting for lunch tomorrow; it gave me a deadline. I wasn't about to show my face without a letter in hand.

It's not as though I haven't had tons of stuff and stories to tell you about or that I haven't had the time to write. It's more that travel—the coming and going and changing and adjusting to time, place, beds et al produces a kind of disconnect in me re my everyday life. It always lasts longer than anticipated. Instead of things running around in my head that I'm dying to tell you and to write about, there's kind of a vacuum. The task of getting back into my Ottawa life predominates.

At the centre of this reorienting myself to Ottawa is my *body* and my *friends*. I simply have to get back to the Carleton gym, to yoga and to massage with Pam on a regular basis. I simply have to reconnect with friends in Ottawa. And I have to re-establish some sense of order in the house, after a long absence. So all this has been going on since we arrived home on March 11, at 3 a.m.,

having left the Yucatán the previous day at 11:30 a.m., looking and feeling like frail ancients about to expire.

We didn't expire! Gil is fine, except for hot flashes (hormones), which he tolerates very well. I've settled in and down, have my body and my friends back. It's 5 a.m.; we were supposed to drop in on out-of-town connections last night, but I begged off and went to bed very early instead. So here I am, sweetie pie, finally writing to you. It feels good, very good.

We decided when you were in San Miguel to stop writing letters beginning of July so our energies would get focused on editing and publishing. Too easy, we agreed, to get diverted by our CP and never take hold of the practicalities, the hard work of trying to publish. Right now the idea of no letters feels kind of scary. Like a drought, like this vacuum I've been in during most of March. We'll have to discuss further; maybe we'll decide to correspond once a month instead of every two weeks—like a gradual reduction of a potent drug (here I appeal to your addictions persona) instead of stopping cold turkey.

I realize how much is lost when stories or incidents are not recorded. Mexico has become sort of a blur by now, a lovely one, with a few memories that stand out. Feeling so much at home in San Miguel in our fourth year there, in our house on Calle Nueva, with our friends and a growing number of connections (overwhelming at times); sitting on a park bench in El Jardin almost daily; playing tennis on Sundays with our gang of six; drinking in the sun and the cobblestones and the stunning colour of everything; eating away in delicious restaurants (nothing to compare in Ottawa) and getting fatter; reading books I would never get to in Ottawa, with Ellen as my

informal librarian (introduced me to Primo Levi). I've always yearned for a sense of community, and, strangely enough, other than in the women's movement, I've found it in San Miguel.

Then, Oonagh, there's the significance of you and Christopher coming to visit, for the second time, while we were in San Miguel. It was sheer joy having you there and coming and going freely at will—thank God you and I are so alike re separateness and togetherness, re ways of being hospitable, re not staying together. You are the only friend I have who is in sync with me about all this stuff, brazenly. The *brazen* is important because I suspect lots of women feel the same way but don't dare to act accordingly.

Gil thrived on organizing Christopher's poetry reading; he is a natural organizer. The poetry reading itself was superb, a real pleasure. And you "guys" and our friends made connections, so there's more knowing on all sides, which is a gift. Of course my check-in idea that night at the Johnsons' was somewhat less than memorable. Jeffrey now makes sarcastic remarks, humorously, about check-ins being group therapy.

Our day in Mexico City with you was more than we ever anticipated. Cozy hotel (forget the name); wandering around Zocolo Square with throngs of people packed in like sardines on hugely crowded streets; eating at the Holiday Inn rooftop restaurant (to Gil's political chagrin) with that remarkable view of the square; selecting safe taxis (at hotels); dinner at that wild, noisy, outdoor café. And much more. I felt so at home with you and Chris, loved, nurtured and protected. Thank you for that. It was a memorable day in my life.

I definitely do not like the idea of your not coming to San Miguel next year because of St. Petersburg and/or other plans. As you know I convert all good experiences into annual rituals, so let's rethink the possibilities.

Then our week at Rio Yucatán with Ruthie and Karen. A joy as always with our two daughters. With lots of catching up, fun, bursts of laughter, playing Upwords et al. Ruthie had us in stitches mimicking Spanish, which she hardly knows but is beginning to study; Karen catches us up on all the hot scoops in the media. We ate as if starved, all kinds of fish I never touch at home. Gil and I paid for our recklessness the last two nights of our stay, vomiting half the night, each in turn. The kids were fine.

Karen, our couch potato, was into tennis this year (never say die); Ruthie began playing last summer, so for the first time we had a Levine foursome playing doubles. Playing games—not just volleying. We loved it, all four of us, one parent and one kid against other parent, other kid. Real tennis. Never thought we'd see the day.

For next year, I wouldn't tie our foursome in with the Yucatán. Too much travel for me. Hopefully, the kids can work out another time, but it is complicated for them in their busy lives. Luckily we're all wedded to a repeat; we all love the foursome. Thank God for that.

Ruthie turns out to be the most energetic one of our gang, and the most active, athletic. She gets up early in the morning, swims in the chilly outdoor pool, walks a mile or more on the beach, meets us for breakfast looking absolutely marvellous. Like a wholesome ad for a vacation or retreat.

Now to the present, to Ottawa. We're all going to Toronto end of April for the launch of Karen's new children's story, *Hana's Suitcase*. A very exciting event for us. Fumiko (children's centre curator in Japan) will be there, arranged for by Hana's brother, George, who lives in Toronto, has money and is very generous. Karen has dedicated her book to Gil and me. Imagine. We are thrilled and proud.

And, beat this, she's just been given a Peabody award for her CBC documentary "Murder in the Neighbourhood," about a man murdering his wife, told from the perspective of neighbours who tried to intervene. Amid the gloomy predictions re what is happening to radio, this is great news. Despite the hours of travel, I will fly (literally and figuratively) to this presentation. Am I getting boring as the proud parent?

Ruthie and Larry's Daniel and I are becoming real friends too. Good thing I lived this long. He's still struggling at school, but I don't much care. He's developing on other fronts and turning into a thoughtful young man. So be it for now.

One other piece of info. Donna has been nominated for a Woman of Distinction award. So some of us, from envisioning group and Lanark County Interval House are going to the expensive Y dinner (90 bucks) to cheer her on. Donna herself has very mixed feelings re being nominated. Not me. I think the more awards for women the better. The more public exposure, the more some people will realize the world needs, badly needs, our talents. Donna is one of my favourite feminists.

Have to eat, shower and go to dentist. May write more before lunch on Friday. Good to be back on track with you, Oonagh. Good to be seeing you tomorrow. Good to have you as a dear friend!

March 29, 6 a.m.

More to say, more to write—that vacuum in my head is fast disappearing. Jane and I had a fascinating exchange re human behaviour, what we do with "attachments," how she maintains distance at times with her closest friends, how Eva and I were mutually needy in our relationship (more in the later years, not so much when younger) and so forth. Jane then turns to me and says (as she has done humorously before), "How come you, for instance, don't invite me to Mexico ?" (Serious this time). Good question to a good friend! I bumble a bit and say, "But you'd have to stay somewhere else, like Oonagh and Christopher do." "Fair," says Jane, but I know she's short of money. Not at all simple in terms of friendship and sharing and taking care of one-self. The strength of our connection is that we can say the unsayable and then pursue all kinds of directions in exploring the possibilities. Jane and I used to consult weekly, for years, in the lobby of the Carleton gym, re issues involved in feminist counselling, getting stuck in the counselling process, etc.

Then there was the morning Gil had a meeting of the Canadian Dimension dinner committee at Botanica. He had an early hospital appointment for prostate stuff, so I let people in, and he got back a half hour later. I wondered afterwards if the small group (five or six), who have worked together for several years, asked about his hospital visit. "No," he said. I think I had mentioned to them that he was at the hospital. Anyhow, the point of all this is that no one in the group, or Gil, spoke of the cancer or the treatment. And it seemed so strange, so detached, so masculine. It's not that I, or Gil, think a hospital appointment is necessarily a big deal; it's not. But there's something less than

okay about proceeding with a meeting as if nothing is happening to people personally. Thank God for the women's movement and consciousness-raising and check-ins.

Gil had put dishes, cutlery and bagels out for the committee. He prepares a mini-breakfast for them. I didn't pinch-hit and someone finally went into the kitchen and got things together (the one woman on the committee, I suspect). I was conscious that any "good" wife would have been more hospitable, more ready to serve in place of her husband. That little vignette will undoubtedly reinforce my already questionable reputation as the wife of an endlessly tolerant, easygoing husband. What a myth!

Terminado, finito. I'm so glad we're meeting for lunch today; I've missed your presence since coming home. I need you around more consistently. But as Jane said, attachments are more complex than they appear.

<div align="center">

With much love,
Helen

</div>

P.S.I didn't even mention the Passover massacre in Netanya, in Israel. I am seething and scared. What in hell is to be done about the killing, about peace? As you say, Oonagh, parallels with Ireland. It is unbearable for me to have men "running" the world. Women are not saints, but somehow I imagine the killings would decrease, the talkings would increase, more compromises would happen if women were in charge.

Oonagh

Monday, April 8, 2002, 11 a.m.

Dearest Helen,

Once more in the kitchen with the door to the balcony open
so that I can hear the rain and the birds. My sort of weather; the
earth smells like Irish earth, so it's as if a switch has been turned
on in my memory brain cells. The mountains, the sea; picking
primroses and violets for my grandmother. She would order me
to go to the woods, and depending on the season, I would pick
flowers or beech nuts. She would then roast the nuts and eat
them.

Chris is out, so no pounding of feet or typewriter to disturb
the quiet. Considering I didn't sleep very well last night, I am
fairly relaxed and positive. Can't believe how up and down I am.
It's not despair; it's sort of a numbing feeling, emotional and
physical exhaustion, not wanting to be the generic caregiver ever
again. But what an amazing, fulfilled life I have had with a role
that came so naturally to me. And what is next? More important,
is there a next?

John Dourley, a Jungian analyst, whom I went to for a
year twenty-four years ago, suggested that as I had begun the

mothering role at such an early age, and it was so ingrained in my psyche, he wasn't sure if I could or would survive without it. At the time he said it, I felt so overextended in that nurturing role. I thought to myself, Oh yes, well, just watch me. Well, dearest friend, here I am, finally able to breathe a little more freely, relieved beyond belief that the women at Amethyst will be well served without me, and that Aaron and Helen are both on their path of independence with the occasional blip that we all go through. And yet, who am I and who am I going to be without those precious roles that gave meaning to my life? I feel I am once more on a major journey.

On the phone the other day, I felt so utterly understood by you. You are truly a gift to me, Helen. Even the words you said were the words I had used to describe to Chris what I felt was happening.

Sunday, April 14

Oh Helen, Helen, I feel so excited, relieved, satisfied when I finally get down to writing; but getting there, to actually put words on paper, is so painful, and sometimes, as now, more difficult and painful than other things. I still have not worked out why, if the act of writing satisfies me so much, I can't just go with the flow. Today I have to force myself to write to you, and I know that in an hour's time, I will hug myself with delight at having achieved yet again another letter to you, despite not wanting to write. I'm amazed when I can do this, feeling the way I do this morning. And I think of your Karen and her writing *Hana's Suitcase*. There are some sentences that are so painful to read that I found myself putting the book down, weeping and then returning to it. I wonder how Karen felt as she wrote it. Having said

that, I think of Anaïs Nin's remark that "we see others as we are, not as they are"! Methinks there is a lot of truth in that saying.

I started writing this in my room but am now in the kitchen and Chris is having his weekly bath! He showers six days a week, but on either Saturday or Sunday, he has a bath. And I mean has to. The world could be falling down around our ears; Chris must have his bath. It drives me nuts! How petty, you think, if that's all she has to complain about. It's not that I care whether he has a bath, it's the fucking predictability of it all. When he and I were children, we had a weekly bath because of a shortage of hot water; because that's how it was in those days in England and Ireland. He is now sixty-eight years of age, and without thought he continues to reenact his childhood, as we all tend to do, some of us more than others. In the case of baths, I have them when I want them. However, to be fair, I do have my little quirks also. Such as always making sure there are potatoes in the house, whether we eat them or not—internalized famine stuff; and that's not my childhood memories, but my great-great-grandparents. I suppose like Chris and his great love of klezmer music.

I want to get back to the whole caregiving thing. Talking after bridge the other day with you and Christel got me thinking again. Now, not sure where to begin. How about, I do not feel or think that I need to invest emotionally with men as much as I do with women and children? When I invited Chris's oldest friend, Anthony, over for six days from England, as a surprise for Chris's sixtieth birthday, it worked out very well. I didn't feel obliged to do anything, and even with Clare, a man who is an old friend of mine rather than Chris's and who came to visit, I didn't feel pressured. But if Judy, the wife of Clare, had come, they would

have stayed in a hotel, and we would have met them for a meal, and the whole visit would have been very controlled by me. I like Judy very, very much, but I get exhausted with the amount of emotional energy I put into our friendship, hers and mine. No, that's not true; it's just the presence of a woman; I automatically get into more of a nurturing role, giving more of myself, or thinking I have to give more of myself; something about expectations.

My mother expected me to be there for her. She confided in me a lot when I was young, about my father. She would say that I was the only one he would do anything for, including stopping drinking if I asked him to; my alcohol and drug training began there! Anyway, I do think the whole nurturing thing around women and children began early. It's not that I don't nurture men; it's that I don't put out the emotional energy with them. Making dinner or breakfast is a cinch without the emotional effort. Does this all sound garbled?

Interesting, though, my son Paul is the only man I give to in the same way as I do to women! I now have to think about that. Off the top of my head, I believe this is more about who he is as a man than it is about me. Am I contradicting myself right, left and centre? Well, I contradict myself! I want to continue this, but I am finding it hard to connect the words I write to the feelings I feel and the thoughts surrounding them. Such as the comment my brother Brian made once: "Remember, Oonagh, we were orphaned at a very early age"! It blew my mind when he said it; I have never forgotten it. A reminder of my childhood, the childhood that I now look at and am grateful for, compared with what Niall and Eithne had. However, when I say that, what have I said? I have been so fortunate in having some great therapists.

All men, who guided me though those awful murky waters into a place where I was finally able to reverse my thinking of "because I had the childhood I had, how could I be anything else but stupid, insecure, nasty, fake, etc." to "because I had the childhood I had, I am who I am and I'm all right"! Hence, my memories changed, and it's not that I forget, it's that I have put more emphasis on the survival skills I learned through it all and on being able to see and understand my mother and my father. To be able to put my childhood and family in context.

I also am very aware that I was loved by my ma and pa and by my grandparents, on my father's side—really loved. I am so glad, Helen, that I was able to meet and have a relationship with my mother as the woman she was rather than the mother she was forced to become. I am glad she lived long enough for that to have happened; it's as if she waited me out, allowing me to catch up with myself as a woman.

I went out to lunch with an acquaintance two days ago, and came away humming to myself, "I'm going to live until I die; I am going to feel pain, joy, anger, peace, whatever until I am on my deathbed." So there's my commitment to you and myself. This woman is into spiritualism in a big way. All-accepting; all-forgiving; all-understanding. Halfway through the lunch, as I became more unaccepting, unforgiving and totally irritated, I thought of you—my wonderful, opinionated, passionate, authentic friend, and friend Marilyn in all her wonderful bitchiness and crabbiness, and I said to myself, thank God (for an atheist, I sure use that word a lot!) I have the most remarkable and amazing women friends who are so true to themselves!

Friday, April 19

They have just put up the tennis nets, so (sort of) summer has come although it's getting down to zero tonight. I am so delighted we are having lunch today.

With my love,
Oonagh xxx

Helen
April 8, 2002

My dear Oonagh,

Gil is out at an Algonquin College[37] meeting. With daylight saving time, the early evening is still light and I want to write. Am sitting in a hard-backed occasional chair, not the big green La-Z-Boy, where I usually hang out to protect my hip and back. Yesterday I could barely move without pain, which scared the hell out of me. After I calmed down, I pondered why this was happening. And decided I need to exercise every day because my feeling of well-being when I do is in stark contrast to what happens when I don't. I've known for ages that I shouldn't be reading, writing, eating, daydreaming, etc., in that soft green chair. But until the pain became truly miserable, I did exactly that. What a creature of habit I am!

I'm now determined to buy a comfortable and appropriate chair, with a reading lamp. I always hesitate to raise such subjects with Gil because he's hell-bent on "making do" and there's no joy in having to argue about why and what and where and how

[37] community college

much. It drags me down and I lose interest and pleasure in the whole prospect and move on to other things. However, when my health is involved, there's little choice but to engage in the process. Jane said to me today, "Why don't you just go out and buy the chair and lamp?" I never have, for all kinds of ridiculous reasons connected to early family conflicts and to the invisible rules in our marriage. It's been much better since we moved to Botanica, but even here stuff wears out or is no longer appropriate and I begin to see the eyesores. If we had no money or if finances were tight, it would be no issue, not at all. But given our more-than-comfortable circumstances, it all seems so insane. Gil and I are absolute opposites re money. Ah, what we didn't know about each other before marriage and about historic family patterns. No wonder the whole world is seething with wars and conflict; if we can't get it together as two seventy-eight-year-old adults in one little family, why are we so shocked by the global family?

I loved our brief exchange about Advil on the phone today. Me thinking it was a huge decision to take one last night (my first), you thinking I was nuts and having taken two yourself; both of us conscious of my having tried different kinds of drugs over many years to deal with depression, insomnia and God knows what else. And me periodically resorting to Valium or sleeping pills, casually, intermittently. In fact, feeling atypical for not being on all kinds of other medication like many women my age. Early family patterns emerge over and over again; taking even an aspirin was big time for my mother; my father disliked and distrusted and avoided the medical profession. Ho, hum . . . so what else is new?!

April 10, 2002

It's the middle of the night, and I'm wide awake. Fell asleep listening to *Ideas* (begins at 9 p.m.). They're broadcasting a series on Simone Weil. Fascinating! It's the first *Ideas* program in ages that I've bothered with because for the past few years they've done mostly boring, uninspired stuff. I used to listen religiously before that; it was one of my favourite programs.

Did you hear Eleanor Wachtel interviewing Carol Shields on Sunday? Very interesting. Carol said her new book *Unless* is her most feminist work, that she is, at this stage of life, more outspoken re feminist ideas. For example, "I count beans," she said, meaning that she is always checking how many women are present or absent in any given situation of authority or significance. I was pleased to hear of another bean counter. I've been one for years. I always remember, having called a friend years ago when I was in a snit re women's non-representation and having been told by her, in a condescending manner, that "I don't count." Which made me feel small and trivial for being a bean-counter kind of feminist.

I think Carol Shields must be very ill, perhaps dying. She didn't attend the recent tribute for her in Toronto where all the beloved Canadian authors, i.e., Atwood, spoke of her and her work. Seems to me that women tell more truths at the end of life. My mother did, just small bits of truth, but significant all the same. I had the feeling that Shields was doing likewise by becoming more outspoken as a feminist.

I have so much to tell you, Oonagh. So much joy and pride re Karen, the Peabody, her book, and her plain old, delicious old unpretentious self. And about Ruthie and her kids who seem to

be emerging in interesting and hopeful ways. Daniel even goes to the Y with his mother once in a while; she knows he likes having her buy breakfast for him there as a bonus, but I say, "Who cares?" It's great that he wants to go. And Rachel continues to wander the world. Her latest shocker is from a Thai island where she and her friend, Eden, went snorkeling with *sharks*. Ruthie and I both decided that was going too far. I remember from way back the pleasure I took in shocking my parents. Did you indulge?

The other important thing I want to write about is your retirement, the search for meaning (Viktor Frankl), and the ups and downs of leaving a busy, focused, structured life. Enjoying the marvellous relief and freedom of it all, but then sensing a vacuum, an emptiness that can be disorienting. Predictable in a way, if you decide not to resort to mere busyness to ease fears and fill the day. I remember being depressed for a few months after I retired and then slowly beginning to find my way. You are much better at taking hold and reaching out than I am, so the prognosis is good, Oonagh. I do believe that leaving space and time, even if it produces anxiety, can lead to new parts of yourself emerging. That last sentence sounds preachy. It's me reaching back into some of my own complicated experiences, wanting to connect with this new chapter in your life. I think I prefer talking to you about this stuff, not writing.

I have to tell you that I've been horribly constipated since returning from Mexico, not a new problem, but none of my usual "tricks" are making an ounce of difference. I'm conscious of wanting to be in good shape for Karen's book launch in Toronto, and I'm starting to feel crummy, crummy enough to call my

doctor and see what's cooking, or not, and what is to be done. God, how I hate going to doctors, and God, how I resent my life being disrupted by my nonfunctioning gut. But here I go, and I hope she will have some simple remedy instead of recommending a colonoscopy or any other instruments of torture.

I was beginning to feel like a Pollyanna with all my recent, unusually positive experiences and positive letters. Forget that, Oonagh. When potential illness strikes, I am not a happy camper. I have been known to magnify minor symptoms into major catastrophes; I'll try to keep the lid on this one.

This is it, Oonagh. A shorter letter than usual.

> With much love,
> *Helen*

Helen
April 24, 2002

My dear Oonagh,

Ralph Benmergui is taking over for Shelagh Rogers this morning on CBC One. Such a smart-ass, so cutesy, the epitome of all the characteristics I find objectionable in a man. He's interviewing Karen and Fumiko re *Hana's Suitcase* between 11 a.m. and noon today. He'd better do a good job or I'll strangle him.

Joan called the other day and we talked about Israel, anti-Semitism et al. Mistake, mistake over the phone. I'm getting more and more impatient re debates that are made to sound like ordinary conversation. We were both doing it. I have to remember that I need and want to explore, to listen fully and be listened to fully. And respectfully. It's hard to hold on to in many situations. But when an issue or topic is close to the bone, it's the only possible way to truly communicate and sometimes to learn from one another. Or go away thinking, pondering anew. It's what I love about our friendship, Oonagh. Let's not ever lose it.

May 14, 2002

I can't remember what interrupted my writing to you, but it's

three weeks since then and so much has happened in between. Your retirement tea; Karen's book launch; two weekends in Toronto; involvement almost weekly as resource person, along with Rosemary and Shirley to staff of Lanark Co. Interval House, where problems are escalating with the board. Then Donna's Women of Distinction evening; two sets of Toronto cousins visiting Ottawa; Faith's farewell dinner (is driving across Canada with Gerd); and joyously, oh, so joyously, giving copies of *Hana* to friends and other people whom I encounter in my daily wanderings and involvements. This has been a rich period in my life, and I don't want to forget the very special moments that have meant so much to me.

Cousin David, Gil's side, gave me this quote last night: "There are those who listen and those who wait to speak." The latter about debating, the former about exploring; I loved it. There are so many great quotes that I've loved and lost through the years. Our CP helps me hold on to some of them. I wonder if anyone will be interested in the tons of paper and writing and articles, in storage, untouched, that I've accumulated? My kids will be interested and curious to a point, and perhaps driven to wade through some of the stuff, minus the articles and books and SSW archival material. It would be endlessly time-consuming and they could easily wear out in the attempt.

Phyllis Chesler has just come out with a new book, *Woman's Inhumanity to Woman*. From a review in *Women's Review of Books*, May 2002, "Chesler argues re... a wider and deeper pattern of women behaving competitively, aggressively and destructively toward other women." She also believes that denial of women's "inhumanity" to other women is basic to the women's movement:

"minimizing and denying woman's sexism is what grounded an entire liberation movement, at least psychologically" and "as feminist women, we knew that we were doomed without sisterhood so we proclaimed it, even in its absence."

"The three central chapters of the book focus on mother-daughter relationships"—should be interesting. Reviewer is Marilyn Frye, whom I trust.

Chesler is, by reputation, said to be impossible (known from involvement in Canadian conferences). I think some of her work was groundbreaking—*Women and Madness*, and *With Child: A Diary of Motherhood*. Just from the review, my response is, So what else is new? Women's lives and relationships are riddled with paradox everywhere you look. Most of us are starved for nurturance, significance and respect, for ownership of our own lives and separate adult selves. I would hope that Chesler has contextualized women's behaviour. Think I might read the book, will suggest it to my book group. Our envisioning group might want to ponder its implications too.

Oonagh, now that you've ended at Amethyst, how are you going to stay rooted in feminism? Or do you think the feminist you is strong enough and clear enough that nothing can budge it? I need my groups to keep me thinking, questioning and seeing. I can't do it alone or even with friends. I need both the sustenance and the provocation of the "sisterhood" and of the few journals still around. And the books. But I know, especially in my old age, that my passion could diminish amid all the other essential adaptations and preoccupations. I'm a feminist to the core, but I don't want it to get blurred and diluted at this stage as I ponder ongoing issues of maintenance of the body, mobility and

quality of life. Is retirement making any difference for you re how you think about this stuff?

One episode I want to tell you about is a party Gil and I went to a few weeks ago. One of the left-wing gatherings that Gil often goes to alone. At Geoff and Jane's house, both good people who have preserved the human touch that I look for these days in people. I knew it would be a big, noisy, talky, political evening, but I was game. Wow! I had forgotten what it feels like to function in this kind of atmosphere. I knew a handful of people there, the wife of someone who used to work with Gil (she was probably as dazed as I); Judy, whom I like but only exchange pleasantries with in a crowd; an old-time Ottawa feminist, Katherine, who recognized me, and we did a catch-up; Rosemary who has preserved personal/political connections better than most; and a few other familiar faces.

But oh, my God, reminiscent of all those years and all those meetings and "socials" and "parties" when I tried so hard to fit in. The lovely part of this experience was that I wasn't trying to fit in or to be "one of." It was just a visit to my past, something I wanted to do for and with Gil. Thank God I have learned to fit into my own skin and ways of being and thinking. It feels very good!

May 15, 2002

Guess I could have mailed my seven pages, but it felt so right when I finally began writing to you again that I wanted to continue. So typical of me—hard to begin anything, then once engaged, involved, I almost can't keep up with myself.

Gil and I went to a play last week at Arts Court called *Westray, the Long Way Home*, commemorating the tenth anniversary of the

Westray mine disaster in Nova Scotia. I'd only been to Arts Court a few times, often found their offerings disappointing. Had no great expectations, but was infuriated by Westray when it happened and then reinfuriated when the senior decision makers got off scot-free. The play was presented by Two Planks and a Passion Theatre Production (what a mouthful!) and financed by United Steel Workers of America. I expected some kind of rah-rah, join-the-union play.

It was instead one of the most moving pieces of theatre I have seen in a long while. Simply, in the best sense of the word, and authentically written, focused on a family and a prodigal sister and two miner friends, acted superbly by all but especially Martha Irving as the wife. I was moved to tears more than once. There weren't many people in the audience, in the small unpretentious theatre, but you could have heard a pin drop and everyone jumped to their feet at the end. For me, the play represented what good theatre is all about, a rare moment.

I had a lovely experience in my yoga class recently. Pat, one of the older women whom I rarely talk to, has a daughter who is a passionate cyclist. She was trying to find for her daughter a Wheelwomen of Canada T-shirt—Wheelwomen of Canada is the presumptuous name of our wonderful, mostly local biking group in Ottawa. She had seen my friend Traute wearing the T-shirt in class. Traute referred her to me, and I contacted Joan, who remains at the centre of things in Wheelwomen. There were no more T-shirts or sweatshirts to be found.

I had bought two of the T-shirts years ago; they were hanging in my cupboard, mostly used during our annual bike trip in Prince Edward County. So I gave Pat the turquoise one for her cycling

daughter. She offered to pay, but I explained how absolutely pleasurable it was/is for me to be able to pass this kind of offering along to an ardent young woman cyclist.

Which reminded me of another story— a biking story too. When, the day before a bike trip years ago, I picked up my very precious Mercier bike from the repair shop for the umpteenth time and it broke down again. I was on Patterson Avenue, near Bank Street, and I sat down on the curbstone (my knees could bend in those days) wondering what the hell to do. Along came a cyclist, male, asked if I needed help. So I told him my tale of woe. He, a complete stranger, said he was experienced with bike repairs, lived across the street, would be glad to fix my bike and bring it back to me in his truck by midnight. So I gave him my bike, and went home by bus. Gil thought I was out of my mind, that it was a scam and I had been duped. His scenario hadn't even occurred to me.

But my bicycle "prince" did appear before midnight and the bike worked like a charm. I was enormously grateful. Offered him a bottle of wine, sensing he would be insulted by money. He refused the wine, accepted my heartfelt thanks and simply said, "Just pass on the good deed to someone else." It was like a kids' fairy tale or morality tale without all the disguises and frogs turning into royalty.

I tell you this because the T-shirt gift felt something like the moral of the bicycle story. Do you think I would have made a good nun, Oonagh? Don't bother answering that rhetorical question. Given my historically troubled relationship to any kind of authority, to taking orders from anyone, the answer is clear.

I was late for my yoga class on Friday, before we met for lunch at the Green Door. As I walked into the large room at the Hintonburg Community Centre, I saw the class in a different way. Everyone silently lying on mats in all directions on the floor, lights very low, sweet gentle music, only Thelma, the instructor, speaking softly. It was a beautiful and touching sight, the absolute antithesis of the noisy, polluted, pornographic, violent world around us. A touch of perspective, which is why I always want to sit toward the back of any theatre or auditorium.

Class that morning was hard work, especially for me, but as always wonderfully relaxing. There were hilarious moments. Thelma had us working in twos at one point. Barbara and I, two of the klutziest, were paired and of course got all tangled up and didn't know where to put legs, arms, etc. We were in stitches, trying to control the laughter. This is not done in your standard yoga class, losing it and having a hilarious time. Fortunately we're old fixtures in this class and pretty relaxed about our clumsy movements. Also fortunately, Thelma has a sense of humour. She's one of the Crones now. We pulled her in after being involved for years in her yoga classes. Episodes like this remind me why I hang in with the familiar rather than searching for new people, new places. The comfort level with the old familiar offers me a kind of freedom and spontaneity that is precious.

Karen is on a pink cloud these days. Getting daily expressions of recognition and appreciation for *Hana's Suitcase*, by snail mail, e-mail, phone, press coverage, etc. Doors are opening all over the place. She's had a turning point re panicking about public speaking. With the kind assistance of beta-blockers (do you disapprove?), she's beginning to enjoy speaking publicly and is beginning to

say yes instead of no to invitations. One of which is to be on a jury for radio documentaries in Italy, in the fall. We love getting the fallout from her exploits; lots of scoops. She wonders how she'll manage everyday life when her fifteen minutes are over.

I'm going to enclose some stuff and stop here. But as always, dear friend, I am glad to have you in my life. I thought after our lunch the other day, what a joy it is to know, really know, one another in many ways, in all our different contexts. Maybe the reason early friendships among girls/women have a lasting impact is because that's when we spent endless hours together, sharing hopes and dreams and secrets. As a young wife and mother, I had two very close friends in Toronto, Eva and Sophie. We could stay up all night talking, relating, weeping and laughing. When we moved to Ottawa, there was no one to replace them. Just "social life,"whatever the hell that was.

I'm back on track, Oonagh. Will try hard to stick to every two weeks.

Lots of love,
Helen

Oonagh

May 5, 2002, 2:30 p.m., kitchen

Dearest Helen,

Alone. Chris has gone to his poetry group. The sun is shining. I woke up this morning feeling at peace. Each day is so different. Sometimes I can hardly get out of bed, but because I need to move my limbs, I do. My moods are up and down. I think it will take me many, many months to recover, physically and emotionally from the years of feeling responsible, etc. at Amethyst.

It's the first time since I was sixteen that I don't have to worry about having a job, having my own money. Even when I was a stay-at-home ma, I was always thinking of ways of having my own money. Not that Edwin ever said the money he made was his. It always went into a joint account, and I paid the bills and gave him a few dollars for his lunches and cigarettes. But I always wanted my own, not to answer to anyone. When Niall was six months old, a friend of mine and I made batches of hand-sewn suede ties! Can you believe it? We both wanted to buy gifts for Christmas. The fucking things took over our lives, pure sweatshop stuff, and the jerk we were working for paid us a pittance. In the end I refused to do any more. Then when I was in

Oakville, I got into making liver pâté and selling it to restaurants. It was very good liver pâté, but again not much money. Are you laughing? Are you thinking, Oh my God, I don't know this woman at all! After that, I got into early childhood education, was a teacher at a co-op nursery school and then taught in a school for handicapped children. Not much money, but it was my very own.

I do drift on. This was not what I was going to write about. Not sure what I was going to write about. Anyway, getting back to my reasonable humour today. I can't even put my finger on what triggers my moods. Late nights don't help, but we had a late night last night, and I'm okay. A couple of minor things happened.

Sheila Pollock phoned and asked me to play bridge again. I was amazed, as I was truly appalling the last time. When I said something to her about it, she said I just needed more practice. She is kind! And then (this is so stupid, Helen), I was passing a young women's soccer game this morning, and the ball came my way and I kicked it. And the young woman I kicked it to said in an amazed voice, "That was very good!" Am I pathetic or what! So, lovey, I go with the flow as much as I can.

We have been somewhat social the last few days. Went to—get this—the Queensway Carleton racetrack the other night. One of Chris's former colleagues phoned us and asked us if we'd go. And I said yes without consulting Chris. If he did that to me, I'd kill him. But he went along with it, and we managed to have fun (I broke even with my betting). I had three winners.

And yesterday morning, we went out to a farm in Navan and met a friend of Chris's, Glynn, who speaks Russian and goes to

Russia a lot. He used to teach in the Russian department at Carleton. Anyway, when he is in Canada (he now lives in Britain with his Russian wife), he stays with a farmer colleague from the Russian department, Galina Van de Lagemaat. Do you know her? She must be around your age. I felt immediately at home in her company. She grew up in Ukraine, Kiev, went to Holland during the war, had a very scary encounter with the Gestapo. She spoke German, so managed to save the lives of two men who were going to be shot. She married a Dutchman, hence her Dutch last name. I asked her if she was going to write her memoirs—she has had such a story. She's not sure.

Anyway, Galina was lovely, interesting and interested, very interested, in our letter writing. She is going to Ukraine in a couple of weeks for a month, her first visit for years. She phoned the Ukrainian embassy and asked them if she died there would they make sure her body was brought back to Canada! She said they thought she was out of her mind. Anyway, she got the answer she needed; they would!

So, Helen, what about your body and Gil's body when you die? What about memorial services? Have you and Gil written something down?

Chris and I have sort of written what we want—private cremation (cardboard coffins, cheap) and a memorial to our lives, probably in the Unitarian building. We both think it's a lovely, attractive place. Helen is the executor of our wills. Also she will have power of attorney. As for our ashes, Chris wants his to be scattered in Jordans, a Quaker Meeting House in the Chilterns. I'm not sure. The Ottawa River seems okay or Cattigolager Mountain in Ireland. My mother is buried in London (cremated).

Her ashes are there and my father's. I have never been to his, and only once to my mother's, so I don't think it's very important. I still want to, at least, inquire whether I could get a small bench put on Howth Head in memory of my ma. It's walking around Dublin that reminds me of her, not a graveyard. At least she doesn't have a great big heavy stone over her. Eithne got her a rambling rosebush. So her ashes may be in London, but her spirit is in Ireland! Isn't that a real Irish thing to say!

Tuesday, 11 a.m.

As usual, I got interrupted. I would have been shocked if I had written this all in one go. We played tennis again this morning. It is truly magic down there at this time of year.

A number of people have remarked on "how spring has started now that we are back playing tennis." It's nice, so the Ottawa River does seem a good place for my ashes.

David Wiseman is in despair about the continued Israeli/Palestinian crisis and not only with what is happening over there but what is happening among friends and family here. He has lost one old friend and his sister thinks he's a traitor, and he's supposed to be going out to Winnipeg to see her in a few weeks. I do wish he had e-mail, as I would get him to contact Gil. I hope he will go to the Peace Now meeting on the twelfth. It might help a little.

I had lunch with Sheila yesterday, and we talked a lot about it and growing up Jewish in Ottawa and the anti-Semitism. You two would have a lot to talk about, Helen.

I can't help thinking of Ireland and the civil war. My father and my grandfather were on opposite sides, and one night my father very nearly shot his father. My grandmother stepped in

and stopped it. To this day, Helen, there are still family members who don't talk to relatives. A madness, all over land and borders. Is there one country in the world that hasn't had brutal killings to maintain borders? Men, the patriarchy, whatever culture it is, continue the same old way of doing things, as they did thousands and thousands of years ago. To quote the song, "When will they ever learn"; not in our lifetime, dearest friend, or in our children's or grandchildren's lifetime. Like David, I despair and shut off and close my ears to it all. Not for very long, but enough to smell the scents of spring, enjoy tennis, write to you (about it all!), talk to friends, etc. Thank God, I do have that ability and thank God, I don't live in a war zone. I do feel blessed.

I received a short e-mail from your Karen the other day re the "maybe" invite for Paul and Terri to her launch. She is yummy, Helen. The whole tone of her note was loving and charming, matching her amazing, rich voice. We have met only a couple of times very briefly, and somehow I feel I didn't take note of her as I should have. Well, Helen, for the record, I am now taking big-time note of her. I have ordered three more copies of her book and am going to send one to the *Irish Times* books editor to get it reviewed there. Paul and Terri were thrilled with it.

I want to get this posted before I go to Toronto. I find it very interesting how I have yacked on about this and that, and I am hardly talking to Chris over something that happened last night in the Russian class. I changed to his class last week, as I felt the other teacher was going far too fast, and I couldn't keep up. I just felt lost. Anyway, last week seemed okay, but last night I felt she, the teacher, was very impatient and exasperated with me and my inability to pronounce certain sounds. I did well with the short

words, but with more than three syllables, I got lost. At one point, I was near to tears and was going to walk out but didn't. She was also sarcastic and said a number of times to me that "we were not there to invent a new language but to learn Russian." Well, I left feeling shitty. Started talking to Chris about it as we were driving home. He responded by saying he didn't think she was impatient, etc. I was shocked and began getting really upset and asked him how come he wasn't aware of it. The long and the short of it was that, yes, he did notice it but felt that if he supported me, I would stop coming to the class. I don't know about you Helen, but when my reality and my perception are questioned, or worse, denied, I feel crazy. No, that's not quite true. Years ago, I felt crazy but now I just go ballistic, which I have done for the past twelve hours. Tennis was great this morning. I won, I hit those balls *hard*. Anyway, over the past hour, we have managed to make a sort of truce. We go dancing tonight, and I won't go if we are not contented with each other. And I am not going back to the class. I am slowly getting to know the alphabet. A friend gave me a great book. I will buy some tapes and practice with Chris. I am not good at languages and feel very self-conscious. I think I would do better one-on-one.

What a messy page, but there you are, another letter hits the post!

With my love as always,
Oonagh xxx

Oonagh

May 21, 2002
6:30 p.m., the kitchen

Dearest Helen,

The Lady of Shalott
On either side the river lie
Long fields of barley and of rye,
That clothe the wold and meet the sky;
And thro' the field the road runs by.
To many-tower'd Camelot;
And up and down the people go,
Gazing where the lilies blow
Round an island there below,
The island of Shalott.

—Tennyson

Well, isn't this a new way of starting a letter?

Every time I look out at the river on a sunny evening, watching people walk beside it, I think of this poem. It's probably my favourite from my childhood. I had to learn it off by heart for elocution lessons. I was even praised by the teacher once for reciting it the exact way she wanted it. I remember only a few verses now.

We usually go dancing on a Tuesday night, but we're invited to a Croatian folk art exhibit, and Chris really wanted to go. I changed my mind about going at the last minute, so here I am, sitting at my favourite writing place, contented with the world, or with my world.

I had a great sleep last night; woke up refreshed, played tennis; it was cool, but oh, what a bit of heaven it is! I think I will suggest to whoever (my Helen?) that my ashes go into the Rideau River opposite this kitchen and just beyond the tennis courts. Some of the most contented moments of my adult life have been when I play tennis early in the morning. By the river and at this time in the evening, the scene is magic for me. All this glory of the countryside without moving out of my habitat. We used to live on First Avenue, which was great, but the house needed a lot of work, and gradually there were only the two of us, so we decided to move. This was the only house we looked at, and we both loved the view of the river, so we said yes after a ten-minute look around. The house itself had, and still has, a number of defects, but we have the view of the river. Well, dearest friend, nearly two pages of babbling on about this is enough.

I thought of you a lot this weekend. I wanted to phone you, but decided not to. I'd love to know how it was with Daniel. I hope it went so well for you, Helen. Sixteen-year-olds, no matter how nice they are, are not the easiest of visitors. When Aaron decided to leave home a couple of months ago and came down here, I didn't mind, as it was a spur-of-the-moment decision, and I don't have to worry about it. But if he were to tell me he was coming for the weekend, I would become anxious. Mind you, if

anyone else told me they were coming, I'd react the same way. I am not an easygoing woman. Are there such things!?

About Phyllis Chesler's new book. I certainly find myself reacting to her saying how aggressive and destructive we are toward one another. Not sure what she means when she says that (read the book, say you!), but we don't kill each other; we don't rape each other; we don't destroy each other's home and murder each other's children. The wars we have between ourselves are civil wars, in the truest sense of that word. What say you, Helen?

Wednesday, May 22, 6:30 p.m.

Chris has gone out to his Russian class. I find this a wonderful time to write. The sun continues to shine on the river and couples are playing tennis. And the house is quiet, the kitchen is tidy, and I am at peace, somewhat. Just received a very charming note from our new next-door neighbour saying how sorry she was that the music was loud last night. We had written them a note telling them it was noisy, saying unfortunately the walls were not soundproofed enough. Anyway, nothing like saying something straightaway, rather than fuming and expecting them to know. I do like being on good terms with my immediate neighbours. We have a retired man, Steve Gannon, who takes care of our house when we're away and looked after the cat. It died in September of last year, so we don't have to worry about that when we go to Russia. He takes in our mail and checks up on the place. We do the same for him. That's what is called neighbourly, village-like. And then there's the Somali man at the end of the block who owns the store where I copy your letters; and the woman Bernadette from Mauritius who works at the post office where I

buy the stamps and post your letters; and my doctor is on Rideau Street, and my dentist is across the bridge in New Edinburgh; and we get the most marvellous bread from the French baker; and when we can't think of anything else, we go to the Lebanese restaurant and buy shawarmas. And then there are all the women and men who walk by the tennis courts on their way to work and remark how pleased they are to see us once more! And the three Chinese women from the embassy who do Tai Chi just beside the courts and smile and wave at us. Do I sound maudlin? Sentimental. I, more than Chris, love the neighbourhood. The idea of walking to work, hopping on buses (I love public transport) and, of course, walking. I got on a bus on Bank Street today, and for minutes I thought I was back in Dublin as a child. I use the car less and less, and generally if I can't get things in my own neighbourhood, I don't bother getting them.

Having said all that, we do have a car, and Chris is great at running me up to the Green Door, delivering books, etc. So I really have the very best of both worlds—choice. How about that, dearest friend, a whole page on my neighbourhood. That is not what I thought I was going to write about.

Monday, May 27

Alone, the kitchen. Once more alone to write to you in the quiet. Chris has again gone to learn Russian. He gets better each day, and I have lost interest. But I do have to get back to it, at least learn the alphabet so that I can wander around on my own. I have no idea what it's going to be like as Chris is going to be very busy and I will have all the time in the world. But if I am not comfortable going out on my own, it could be a disaster. So learn

some Russian I must. As soon as Chris gets all his information regarding course time, etc., I will write to our contact, Vadim, and make some requests such as "Do please find me a feminist who speaks English" or "Introduce me to a group of like-minded women." And I will write a list of what sort of women I would want in the group—women who are opinionated, feminist, political, humorous, passionate, sensitive, interested in discussing, not debating, play bridge and speak English! I think I dream a little too much!

About debating. I was telling daughter Helen last week, at lunch, about a discussion you and I had many, many years ago, probably sitting at the same table in the Green Door. You might not remember it, but often it comes back to me. Not so much the discussion itself, but how I felt when we had finished, and how at peace I was when I walked home after it all. We were discussing our thoughts and feelings about Elspeth Cameron's very honest account of her divorce and her new lesbian relationship[38]. You thought it was wonderful and very courageous of her, and I thought she had written it too soon and would regret what she wrote in a year or two. I was all ready to have a good argument with you, Helen, but you didn't let that happen. We ended up talking, reflecting, wondering together, thinking and pondering what the other had said. It was one of the longest lunches we ever had, and I came away delighted, excited and totally in love with you, knowing something major had happened in the tone of the discussion, and at the time not sure what. I remember feeling

[38] *No Previous Experience: A Memoir of Love and Change*, Elspeth Cameron (Toronto: Penguin Canada), 1998

very passionate about my thoughts on her writing the book, and usually, if I feel that strongly about something I avoid discussing it with anyone because I don't want to debate and argue my points, their points, etc. But you, dearest friend, didn't do that. You listened carefully to what I had to say, and you responded in your own very thoughtful way, and I remember the great feeling of relief I had when we looked at each other, saying at the same time, "That was a great lunch." Do you remember? It matters not, but I do want you to know how important it was to me.

Helen (daughter) expressed envy that I have such a friend. She had a friend she could talk to about everything without debating, but then the friend changed, and Helen changed and they lost that particular way of being with each other. Maybe they will get it back one day. Maturity must have something to do with it!

Now on to another topic. This time about my sister Eithne. When I phoned her on Sunday, she was very despondent over a situation with a new friend. We spoke about it for a while, went on to other things and said goodbye. The next day, Monday, I began to think about our conversation and decided to phone her again and talk some more about it. Well, Helen, she couldn't believe it. It was as if I had given her a million dollars or whatever. Her words to me were "Well, you are something else, Oonagh. Imagine you taking the time to think about me. I appreciate it so much, Oonagh, and I will sleep well tonight." I was so shocked and amazed at her response. Such a small thing for me to have done, but what a reward! We spoke a little on Sunday about her son Paul, whom she gave up for adoption when he was three months old. He was thirty-four on Sunday. She's

wondering what he was/is like. Is he married? Has she got grandchildren that she doesn't know? She does hope that one day he will find her. She has put her name in a registry. Brigid[39] died this time last year, and since then Eithne and I have spoken on the phone every Sunday. So we have got to know each other in a different sort of way. Not as much older sister/younger sister stuff, more like two friends.

Wednesday, 7:30 p.m.

I received your wonderfully written May 26 letter today. How on earth can you write so well at 3:30 a.m.? And I was hoping to post this today but didn't. I pottered for too long this morning, had lunch with Joan Wilcox and then felt too tired at 3:30 p.m. to write. Something wrong with this picture! Anyway, I'm going to finish tonight, copy it and deliver it by hand tomorrow.

Much love,
Oonagh xxx

[39] An old friend of Eithne's whom she took care of when Brigid was diagnosed with MS.

Helen

May 26, 2002, 3:30 a.m.!

My dear Oonagh,

One reason I'm up at this crazy hour, writing, is that I slept so much yesterday. Couldn't keep my eyes open after I played tennis (first time this year) in the morning. I think my body was so stunned by the intake of oxygen, both the tennis and the being outdoors for two hours, that it caved in temporarily. Unlike you, I don't ordinarily get much fresh air. All my exercising is indoors; I don't like walking and my biking days are almost over. I'd better hang on to tennis for both the joy of it and the fresh air. Actually had a pretty good doubles game.

I am low status at the tennis club, meaning that I get to play when it's my turn. People are more than tolerant and charitable about my less-than-inspiring play, but it's clear that no one is dying to have me in their game. I'm philosophical about this reality and sit at the bottom of the heap pretty casually. I like the me that has learned yet another of life's lessons. And I'm grateful, truly grateful, to still be playing tennis and breathing gobs of oxygen at seventy-eight.

It was simply gorgeous yesterday—hot sun, cool air and the

lushness of spring rampant at the Experimental Farm, where the courts are located. I love this time of year—the beginnings of growth—the magnolias, the cherry blossoms, the lilac bushes everywhere as I move around the city.

There was a brunch at the tennis club yesterday; it was delicious, almost gourmet, food prepared, of course, by all the good women; with the new social convenor explaining how it all works well because of the people who participate and contribute. I, of course, was one of the non-contributors except for my five bucks (acceptable, but clearly not desirable)—hadn't known about it, but knowing would have made no difference.

A contrast from my feminist friends. Had our book group the other night—Makeda Silvera's *The Heart Does Not Bend*. Food was blah, the house messy, the people interesting, the talk personal and political. My cup of tea. Next time we're doing Phyllis Chesler's new book *Woman's Inhumanity to Woman*—reviewed recently in the *Women's Review of Books*.

Have to get a copy of June's *Quill and Quire*.[40] Karen says there's a great review of *Hana's Suitcase* in it. She's emerging from the high of publication and the Peabody Award, is now beginning to deal with fatigue, having too much on her plate and no time to read. The laughs are giving way to the strain of overwork and over-involvement. Gil drove to Toronto today for a week of meetings, seeing friends, going to a conference on gender and the labour movement (Peterborough), so he will give Karen some relief. He's low maintenance, happy to Gabriel-sit, cook, do joe jobs. I'm high maintenance, Karen says, and I agree. Except in a crisis.

[40] Canadian publishing industry news

It's good being on my own. The silence of the house is relaxing and peaceful. I think I've never been fully at ease with others in my home. Perhaps never learned how, or felt required, to be more domestic and more hostessy than I really wanted or was able to be. We used to have lots more visitors in the early years—parents, siblings, nieces, nephews, friends. Eva once came to our small two-bedroom apartment on Tilbury—with first baby Diane and a trunk—and stayed for a month! What a contrast to now.

Ruthie's son, Daniel, stayed here overnight last weekend. Didn't want to go to the cottage with parents—Ruthie and Larry won't leave him alone overnight at home. I was glad to have him here. And he was easy, a good sport, helpful. So was I! I watched basketball on TV with him. We played Upwords. No organized meals, just food in the fridge. We talked basketball, I gave him my keys, told him only he and Gabriel are allowed to visit overnight. It felt good.

When someone else is staying here, if I haven't lived with them before—i.e., the kids, Eva, Addy, the grandchildren—there's a touch of discomfort. As if I should be doing things with or for the other. I'm like my mother. She would come for short visits and stay in a small hotel close by. I liked it that way. My father in his later years would make an annual two-week visit, staying with us and not talking much to Gil (whom he disliked). So I carried the weight of the visit. I didn't begrudge him these "holidays." He was a lonely old man who through many years had nurtured and adored me. I can barely remember who I was then and how I managed. Or he managed. Or Gil managed. I guess the gender expectations then were so powerful that there was no question about not trying hard to make others feel at home in my home, and ignoring my own

capabilities in the process. Women are expected, generally and globally, to service men. I give thanks to my poor, unappreciated and often unloved Mother for pointing me in alternative directions. Wish she could hear me now.

Granddaughter Rachel comes home the end of May, after nine months travelling on her own in Asia. I'm amazed at her sheer guts, her capacity to hang in with this adventure. At nineteen!

Karen's Michael is in town, phoned. He got me a ticket to the CBC forum he's moderating at the art gallery, with CBC foreign correspondents. I'm going by myself, didn't think fast enough to have him get me two tickets. I'm getting better at doing things alone. I want to learn that freedom, to further detach myself from social expectations. I love companionship and friendship, but I also want to be more comfortable in my aloneness when I'm out in the public sphere and visibly alone.

At the forum, I sat beside a young Irishwoman who told me she loves the CBC. She's from Galway, has been in Canada for about ten years. I was struck that her two sons were involved in this seemingly adult situation. The twelve-year-old lined up at the mike and eventually asked a question, which was whether the flak jackets the foreign correspondents wear as a security measure really work, what they're like, etc. I was impressed. The parents, both of them, were attractive and casual. I thought to myself, are all Irish people good-looking like Oonagh? Such is the trivia of my mind that I indulge these thoughts while listening to grave discussions of world-shaking issues. No introductions, just a fleeting bit of conversation and observation that pleased me. If I hadn't been alone, the connection wouldn't have taken place.

Then to the Green Door to get takeout. No takeout today, as it was the Green Door's free anniversary meal to all comers. So I sat down with a delicious meal, eavesdropped on two young women sitting next to me and again enjoyed my aloneness. Do you think I'm in danger of becoming a recluse? I think not, but there is something to be said for wandering the city solo. It gives you a whole new perspective.

This coming Friday we leave for the Wheelwomen bike trip. I'm driving with Rosemary and Kate. Joan and Christel go together, room together. Addy and I share a room. I couldn't take my bike because three bikes on a rack is dicey and the others had made arrangements. Which wasn't a big deal; I hardly ride anymore. But Joan Taylor couldn't bear this arrangement and generously found one person to take my bike and another to bring it home. Joan T. started the bike trips and is an organizer par excellence.

Monday, May 27, 2002, evening

To continue. Four women playing bridge at the condo. Two hotshots, two klutzes—me and Anne. I get away with a certain amount of klutziness. Anne is a Brit, probably a war bride. So we're gabbing and it's Jeanne's seventieth birthday, which leads to telling our ages. We're all stunned when Anne says she's eighty-five, eighty-six this October. Which puts a whole different perspective on her persona. Among other things, she tells us she rode a bicycle up until a year ago and that she "lost a girl." We went on playing bridge, but later that night I couldn't stop thinking about her. I was reminded yet again that every woman has a story, that the outside is only a surface and how little we human beings know or share about one another.

This is why I love check-ins. You get to know about people's lives; there's less scope for assumptions and judgments. Hence more generosity toward others because the knowing gives you perspective and understanding.

To Ruthie's for supper last night, Michael there too. Interesting how, as the men talked, Ruthie and I became more silent. After the guys left—Larry drove Michael to the Château Laurier hotel—I looked at Ruthie and said, "men" in that loaded, what-is-to-be-done kind of way. Ruthie agreed. There's no dialogue. We used to talk about how women do the shit work of the conversation and ask questions, make linkages, look interested and become almost invisible. I don't do that anymore, but it can make for a bloody awkward get-together.

The rewarding part was that Ruthie and I had a really good conversation about all that stuff. I asked if she thought the guys, including Gil, realized how lucky they are to have us in their lives. I was conscious of how we two were listening and hearing and responding to each other and what the hell is the point of talking without these ingredients. Ruthie is sure Gil knows how lucky he is; you could have fooled me! I prize these moments with my daughter.

I have lots to do before taking off on the bike, or non-bike, trip on Friday. There are twenty-five women on this trip. I'm going to take care to not get overwhelmed. I'll phone you before I leave. You now belong to my required "hello and goodbye before going out of town" group—very special. Take care, my dear Oonagh.

Lots of love,
Helen

Helen
June 19, 2002

My dear Oonagh,

I've just gotten off the phone with you. Your last word was "write." July is almost here, our deadline, our full year of writing letters. And I haven't been doing well these past few months. So—sheepishly, guiltily and somewhat desperately—here I am, kid, back at the ranch and full of stuff to tell you about. Also conscious of how I completely forget about lovely moments, rich connections when the writing stops. What was it Oscar Wilde said about how we kill the things we love??

June 21, 2002

It's early Friday evening. Gil has taken off for the cottage with Chris W. Silence reigns as does my determination to write. Have decided not to answer the phone. I've left a message for you re seats at the CBC forum in the Studio at NAC tomorrow evening. Suggested you call me in the morning.

My neck, shoulders, head are a little better tonight. Late afternoon and evening are the worst times usually—almost as if my neck can no longer carry the weight of my head. No fun having

your well-cared-for and well-exercised body let you down for more than two weeks. All of this happened just after the Wheelwomen bike trip, where I had a marvellous time gabbing, singing, laughing, being wild. I hardly biked, nor did Addy or Joan. We were the three "invalids" (my term; Addy and Joan heartily dislike it).

Mind you, I had a warning during the trip that I was overdoing things. By four-thirty the second afternoon I retreated to my room for the night. Addy brought me a bit of supper, and Christel made sure I was okay. The fact is, I could not, *could not*, handle any more stimulation or face twenty-five women (unusually big trip) over dinner at the B&B.

It was after we left Prince Edward County, heading for home that something snapped in my upper back and pain just flooded through my body. Brief but clear and definite. And then later the aches and pains settled in neck, shoulders and head. My GP guessed it was a torn tendon, which usually takes a few weeks to heal. Said to take Advil. My worry is the osteoporosis that I have ignored and refused to take medication for. Anyhow, if there isn't marked improvement by Monday, I'll return to the GP and ask for an X-ray and an overdue bone density test. With more humility and less defiance, I may even accede to medication.

The upshot of my aches and pains has been a careful rethinking of the part of me I like best—the passion, the intensity, the zaniness, the sheer joy I have when with my feminist sidekicks and with Ruthie and Karen. How to deal with all of the above without knocking my seventy-eight-year-old body for a loop and suffering very unpleasant consequences? Of course it could be said that my hypothesis is ridiculous, with absolutely no basis in scientific fact or reality. Why don't I just listen to my doctor, as

normal people do. Because, say I to myself, I know how my body and my intensities interact, whatever the facts of the case.

I cancelled most of my activities this week to rest and stay relatively quiet. Cancelled the Crones trip to Perth. And the weekend with our feminist envisioning group at Rosemary's cottage, one of my very favourite gatherings each summer. I'm going to have to tone down my excitable nature and try to indulge in fun and laughter for shorter lengths of time. It's clear that I'm overwhelmed by crowds and too much talk, even when I'm thoroughly enjoying myself.

On the bike trip, there were two dinner tables. One was mostly "our gang," women who know one another well. The other table was a mix of many of the women who bike in Europe, Cuba, etc., together, a few of whom are established professionals. We heard, via the grapevine (no gathering of women is without a grapevine), that some of them consider some of us passé radical feminists. I, of course, fit their description to a T.

Have I mentioned that our old neighbours from 1411 Woodward Avenue, where we lived for thirty-six years, dropped in to see us last week? They moved to Owen Sound years ago and more recently to Guelph. Shirley and Jack were/are good, salt-of-the-earth, open-minded people. Shirley and I didn't have a lot in common except kids and motherhood and a need for personal connections out there in the suburbs. But we clearly liked each other. Ruthie used to tell Shirley her teen troubles (very important), and Karen went to their place for lunch when I worked at Ottawa CAS. We were good, caring neighbours. We've seen them a few times over many years, caught up on what's happened to kids, and Shirley's becoming a real estate broker.

This visit was lovely and different. They've been through five years of hell, he with prostate cancer (surgery), heart complications, cataract surgery, she losing her only sister to cancer. They were open and personal, and we thoroughly enjoyed the visit. Took them to La Roma on Preston Street for dinner, came back to Botanica to gab. Shirley is a competitive curler, loves it. Credits me with babysitting her kids and thus allowing her to get involved in curling years ago in Ottawa. I really liked Jack in his new openness. I gave them a copy of *Hana* and we parted as friends. I love these totally unexpected, rich moments in life.

Addy and I celebrated her eighty-fifth birthday at the Château for two nights. We like hanging around the Château lobby, reminiscing and people watching. The Château is part of her Ottawa childhood, as well as mine. Then we ambled up to the Famous Five sculpture on the Hill, in between downpours of rain. Though Addy can't see much (legally blind), she touches and I read the names and the info for her.

I ordered breakfast in our room both mornings. It reminded both of us of how thrilling and how rare it used to be to indulge in room service.

The next day, Addy spent time with Gil, then we visited her sister-in-law in Central Park Lodge. She has terminal cancer, mostly stays in her room, seemed glad to see us. Same age as Addy—a terrible contrast—one woman so sick and immobilized, one so healthy and travelling. Life is not fair!

That night we went to Kate's choir concert, In Harmony plus Womansing. Some marvellous feminist songs, a bit of audience participation, in general an unpretentious atmosphere of women singing about women, which I love. Connections at intermission,

delicious as always. Addy was in her element too; she doesn't have these kinds of opportunities in Montreal.

Left a message for Judy, who may help with the publication of our correspondence. She answered promptly. Sounds organized and reliable. Who wouldn't want to read other people's letters? I certainly would. I'm going to get four letters to her tomorrow morning. Feels good re our CP, though I'm beginning to realize how very complicated confidentiality is in relation to family and friends. No wonder many writers live isolated lives on the margins.

Karen told me to pick up the current *Toronto Life*; Michael has a piece in it about his Catholic (Irish) boyhood in Toronto. Including a wonderful picture of him as altar boy. I found it fascinating, beautifully written, very personal. I think he has a book in him about growing up Catholic. You and Christopher would probably appreciate the article.

This letter has been a catching up at many levels: first of all writing a long overdue letter, then recounting stories I've already told you about at lunch or on the phone (from the beginning we knew gabbing could be our downfall). I don't like to lose our philosophizing, our sharing of ideas, our exploring. It's only when I write regularly that the mix of these elements seems to flow easily.

Now that it's almost July (one year), what will we do without our CP? We've agreed we both want to continue writing letters, but will we have a structure or will we write at random? Big question for me. My assessment of this particular letter is that it suffers from a catch-up mentality because our structure is now weaker (my responsibility, of course).

Please ponder this stuff, Oonagh. Maybe it's all about getting closer to submitting for publication, to dealing with practicalities, to getting something together before you take off for Russia. Whatever the complications, I do not want to lose what you and I have forged with our CP.

Goodnight, dear friend.

Lots of love,
Helen

P.S. Gave Judy my four letters. Liked her clarity, her personal take on things like friendship, and her grasp of confidentiality. She lives next door to Faith so has heard lots about me. God, there are so many interesting women in this world. Oh, and she's young and energetic!!

P.S. Oonagh, do you remember reading Tillie Olsen's *Tell Me a Riddle* and how the old woman with cancer wanted to be left to her own rhythms? This is the excerpt.

Never again to be forced to move to the rhythm of others. For in this solitude she had won a reconciled peace. Tranquility from having the empty house no longer an enemy, for it stayed clean not as in the days when it was her family, the life in it, that had seemed the enemy: tracking, smudging, littering, dirtying, engaging her in endless defeating battle. Being able at least to live within, and not move to the rhythms of others as life had helped her to.[40]

Is this why we're both able to write best when we're alone in the house? I can make all kinds of connections. Can you?

[40] *Tell Me A Riddle*, Tillie Olsen (New York: Dell Publishing), 1956

Oonagh

June 23, 2002
9:30 a.m., the kitchen

Dearest, dearest Helen,

I bawled my eyes out when I read Tillie Olsen's quotation. What an amazing one to end a letter with! I thought of my mother and how she found those last fifteen years of her life, and how at peace she was with her small compacted world. She lived in Cambridge for twelve of those years, and she loved it. She had a small apartment in a seniors' home, lived very simply, just with the necessities of life, very little money, but enough for her needs. She walked every day, sat on benches that were scattered around that beautiful city and talked to whoever came along. Mostly the young people—she loved them and they, I am sure, loved her. She had a very sharp wit. Actually, both she and Dad had great humour, and when they had moments of gentleness together, I remember the quick repartee they had with each other.

I don't know what my rhythms are outside of others. No, not quite true. I think I am somewhat aware of what I would like them to be, as I spend enough time fighting for my space, be it with Chris, friends, children and grandson. Now I'm going to contradict myself by saying yes, I do know what my rhythms are.

And when I stay true to them, I feel so contented. But—a very big but—I also have precious relationships that I want to nurture, and that's where the difficulty is. I think in a previous letter I wrote that I would do well in a monastic setting—a little prayer, a little chat, a little play, etc., although the problem would be fitting in to the community structure and not going with my own rhythms. It wouldn't work. I always envied the men (they were always men) who rang the church bells, calling people to pray. When I was young, I used to imagine what it would be like to be able to summon people whenever you wanted. I thought the bell ringer was more important than the priest, who, after all, needed the sound of the bell to wake him up and wake up the community to go to mass. But then again, I wouldn't want others to feel they had to copy my ways, and I certainly don't want that responsibility. So, Helen, I believe I am a birthright anarchist. I asked Chris how to spell anarchist and he said, "If you are a birthright anarchist, you can spell it any way you want." Smart-ass, eh? And if I am not an anarchist, I am a freethinker, and here's a quote from Penelope Fitzgerald's book, *The Beginning of Spring*. Carol Shields sent it to us a few months ago when she heard we were going to Russia. "I am not an unbeliever, I am a freethinker. As a freethinker I can believe what I like, when I like. I can commit you, in your sad situation, to the protection of God this evening, even though tomorrow morning I shan't believe he exists. As an unbeliever I shall be obliged not to believe, and that's an unwarrantable restriction on my thoughts." So I'm a freethinking anarchist! Oxymoron.

Monday, June 24

Imagine, there are church bells ringing. Usually I hear them only on Sunday. So, Helen my dear, another disjointed letter. I am in the kitchen, the air outside is perfect, Chris is *out* all morning; bliss! We both read Michael's article; it is wonderful and the first couple of paragraphs are riveting. What a bolshie boy he was; what a grand sense he had about him! Is he going to write an autobiography? His writing is so entertaining and open. He certainly brought back memories for me—the incense, candles and the marvellous Latin masses, sung, just wonderful theatre. Men and boys dressed up as women—archaic, but grand once you didn't take it seriously.

Niall, my son in White Rock, was forty last Thursday. Can't believe I have a son that age. I bought him a telescope, as he and Karin live in a house overlooking the ocean. I couldn't have bought him a better gift. He sounded like a kid when he phoned to thank me. I do so love when I get it right. My grandparents lived opposite Dun Laoghaire Harbour, on a hill, and one of my favourite pastimes was looking through my grandfather's old leather-bound telescope at whatever the sea had to offer. So in some ways, it was my own need to imagine Niall with a telescope. They also live on a hill with a big picture window.

Did I tell you that he phoned me a few weeks ago to let me know they have a room all ready for me, overlooking the ocean? I was so thrilled to have an open invitation, and he was very surprised at my reaction. He said he thought I knew I was always welcome. I didn't. What is so nice about it all is that they have no children, and both of them are out all day, plus there is a small kitchen and bathroom and a separate entrance. So I might never

have to see them! And they would never have to see me. I certainly can see myself going there for a week or so on the spur of the moment.

Sunday, July 28

I really am dragging my feet on this one. By now I should have written and posted two letters. I do intend to write one more so that the project is complete. I am finally editing and putting the letters on the computer, which is taking over my thoughts and my time. Since leaving Amethyst, I am not as organized as I used to be, so the hours run into days and the days into weeks, and I'm not getting things done as I used to. You will be horrified to know that I spent quite a bit of our precious time watching the world soccer series! I love the game because all you need is a ball. I think it's a great equalizer, and if I were leader of the world, I would decree that all boys and men play soccer. I would destroy all weapons. I would make North and South Korea sort out their differences on the soccer field, as well as the Ulster Unionists/Republicans, the Israelis/Palestinians, etc. The problem with that is not the players. It would be the supporters. But then if I were leader of the world, supporters themselves would get the chance of playing, so it would be in their own best interest to behave.

My dear friend, having spent many hours thinking about what I would write about my initial meeting with Chris and those very heady days, I have decided not to write about it. Why, you ask. Well, I can't just write about that. I would have to put it in context and that I am not prepared to do in this format. Maybe poems, maybe short stories; maybe write it up, and give it to Paul to make use of it all when I die. One of the main reasons I won't

do it is that I couldn't bear the thought of hurting Edwin; and it would hurt him. He loved me dearly, Helen, in his way. For a while it worked; well, more than a while, and then it didn't, through no fault of his or mine. If I wanted revenge, it would be a great way of getting it, but I don't. I have nothing to punish him for. We have been friends for forty-two years, and I can't imagine not being able to pick up the phone and chat to him about the kids, grandchildren, Eithne (whom he is very fond of, and who loves him) and all the other areas of our lives that we share. I have spoken at length to Chris about it. He has written eight chapters of his autobiography, and although he touches on his two previous marriages and his affairs, he hasn't gone into any major details. Certainly in his poetry he has written about relationships, but somehow it's more subtle. And then there are the children, although for the most part they know about my crazy, creative nutty times; we were all teenagers together! If I were to write about it so openly, I think they would be extremely concerned at the effect it might have on Edwin. Even if the children said yes to it, I wouldn't do it. I do talk about that time to them, and with them, and we laugh, and they tease me about it. Oral storytelling at its best.

When I look back at that time, between the age of thirty-two and forty-four I think, I am so pleased it all happened. I would never be the person I am now if it hadn't—the affairs; the depression; becoming a chaplain at the Unitarian Church; returning in a small way to acting; my job at Rideauwood. It was as if I was at the height of my creative powers; I was! It was a passionate heady time for me; and there was the crash, and with it the shame and despair of having to relinquish my role as

chaplain. I was a very good one, Helen, but obviously not good enough! I introduced vesper services; a mixture of music, readings, candles, poetry. I performed weddings. I have many photos. I was a chaplain at the Queensway Carleton Hospital, there for the atheists and agnostics. I conducted services, the most memorable one being when I introduced myself to the congregation just before I became a chaplain. I called it "Once upon a time." I spoke about my childhood, my children and my marriage. I read favourite poems and had special music played. A friend played the flute; I had flowers and candles (I do love candles). It was truly magic. The building was packed, and for this rather intellectual congregation, very different. I got some marvellous letters after it all, and the service was written up in the church paper. I think I have a copy somewhere. I think that oral tradition is ingrained in my psyche. Mind you, I couldn't do that anymore. I am delighted everything happened. I have great, great memories, and I am delighted to be where I am now. At times when I look back, I can't believe I had that sort of energy. Not only to get through the pain but the joy as well.

I certainly have regrets, mostly about the children. I was not there for any of them during their teenage years. Oh yes, I was physically present, but not emotionally present in the way I feel I ought to have been. I think part of it was that I had adult responsibilities at the age of fourteen. Both Edwin and I had left school at sixteen, and neither of us thought that the children needed guidance, attention, etc., during those years. And although they each have turned those very painful experiences into something positive for themselves, I wish those years had been a bit gentler for them. However, they might not be the peo-

ple they are today. And I am well satisfied, in fact delighted, with the three of them. So, dearest friend, I won't beat myself up too much. I used to say to my mother when she'd tell me what a bad mother she was "But, Ma, aren't you delighted with how I turned out?" And she'd say, "Yes, of course I am." And then I'd say, "So how on earth could you have been a bad mother?" And we'd look at each other and laugh.

The Snowbirds have just flown over. How on earth do people survive bombers flying over their heads day in and day out? I often wonder about Canadians who come from war zones. What do they think and feel when they hear the noise of fireworks on Canada Day. It is now 5 p.m., and I have spent most of the day writing to you, and feeling at peace. Chris and I went for a walk by the river. It was heavenly.

I think I'm going to pop over and drop this off in the office tomorrow. Then I'll phone you and tell you it's there. Big Canada Day Surprise! What a late, late letter.

Much love, and gratitude for your
patience and friendship, dearest Helen,
Oonagh xxx

Oonagh

Monday, July 8, 2002, the kitchen

Dearest Helen,

Well, we did it—a year to the day that I wrote my first letter to you. My pens are slowly running out of ink, so it's just as well we are winding down. I think it was such a good idea to have an end in sight, as I believe if we had left it open-ended, it might have drifted on because we had made the commitment to write to each other, and eventually it could have become a struggle for either one of us, or both of us. Although, dearest Helen, I am not sure what I am going to do with all my bits of gossip and news. I also am aware that I have other writing to do such as poems, short stories, and I would dearly love to try my hand at writing a play for either the stage or TV. Algonquin College offers a workshop on script writing, so when I come back from Russia, I will apply to take it. I do hope that we will continue to write to each other on an ad hoc basis. Certainly I can't imagine not writing from Russia. And then, there is our wonderful deepening friendship that I know will continue with phone calls, lunches and bridge.

As I reread my letters, I am fascinated by what I wrote about, and what I didn't write about. For example, there are many friends

270

I have hardly even mentioned, and it's not as if we haven't seen them over the year; it's just that somehow, when I wrote to you, there was always other stuff. And even when the writing was difficult (it was always difficult), I couldn't just write about whatever. If these do get published, there are going to be friends who wonder why they haven't been mentioned.

I found that out a number of years ago when a man called Aidan McIvor wrote a history of the Irish Navy, the first one ever written. Although my grandfather was mentioned, my father wasn't. I was in total shock for days, even questioning my own memories of my history, such as the fact that my father was liaison officer and was decorated by Spain and Sweden for services rendered when their ships and submarines came into Dublin port. At the time, around 1948, the newspapers described him as the most decorated sailor in Ireland. My brother Brian has all the medals, newspaper photos and articles in a glass case. I hope that one day they will end up in the Irish Naval Museum.

I wrote to Aidan McIvor, who was very apologetic, said he got little or no help from the Irish government (he was British), and that if a second edition came out, he would definitely include my dad. I don't know if that happened. I did go and look up my father's file in Dublin, and although it did have some information, much was missing. Another book came out a few years ago, and again my father wasn't mentioned. I wrote to that author too, even spoke to him, as he lived in Dublin. He was grumpy and more or less told me I should be satisfied that my grandfather was mentioned. I think it still has something to do with the Civil War, which side you were on. My father was in

Irish intelligence during the war; that also could have something to do with it. Plus, he did make enemies.

I can't believe that I've gotten into all this. My last letter to you and again I'm writing about my Irish family. I started with them, and it looks as if I'm ending with them too.

Friday, July 12

Oh, isn't this a great day to be writing to you! King Billy Day, as it's known in Northern Ireland. All those narrow-minded evangelical Protestants marching through the streets of Ulster waving their Union Jacks and beating their drums, singing "God Save the Queen!" When you think of it, it was pretty terrible to partition such a small island, but then, think of the absolute horror when India and Pakistan were divided, again by the British, with thousands and thousands of people massacred. So, dearest Helen, I rant and rave to the bitter end.

Today you are back from your five-day writing retreat. How I look forward to hearing all about it! My week has gone by. There were a few lunches, but more and more, I'm thinking about our visit to Russia. Still haven't got our visas as the embassy needs the original copies of our invitation, and we only have faxed copies. Also, because Chris is staying more than three months, he has to have an HIV test, which takes a week to come back from the lab. Anyway, a lot of bureaucracy.

Saturday, 10 a.m.

Chris has just gone out shopping, and I'm waiting for a phone call from my friend Dorothy Thurley who lives in Oakville. We try to phone each other every couple of weeks—to gossip about the

past and the present and to share our dreams about the future. Our friendship started in the early '70s and has continued on and off until now. We have had our moments (years actually) with each other, but manage somehow to meet up again with promises of fidelity—until the next time! We love each other dearly but are very different. She is bright, humourous and nicer than me! At times over the years, she has felt I was too opinionated, critical and generally a pain in the ass. She and Edwin had a thing for each other at one time, and I think it could have been great for both of them, although they both border on pessimism, so I'm not sure. So there, I have now written about my friend Dorothy.

Imagined my last letter would be reflective, but that's not what's happening. It's going to be the same disjointed ramblings as usual. I have put three of my early letters on the computer to send to a publisher. I would like another one, but as I read over them, I realize I will have to do a lot of editing, which means having to rewrite paragraphs. So I am thinking I will just leave it at three. What do you think? I have written a lot about my children and Amethyst, but most of all I have written about my daily life, and my thoughts, and the major insight out of it all is that my home and my heart is in Ottawa, overlooking the Rideau River. Are you now dumbfounded after all my previous longings about Ireland? Location has always been important to me; sitting here over the past year, watching the river and its surroundings change with the seasons; delight at playing tennis a few yards from the house; on the other side, the bustle of the very manageable city with its French atmosphere and diversity of other cultures; and my friends and neighbours—

all of which together makes Ottawa a place I would grieve for if I decided to live somewhere else.

Having said all of that, I would just remind you, dearest friend, that I am a *freethinker*. On my deathbed, I could possibly believe there is a God. In my nineties, I could decide I need to live in Dublin beside the sea. After all, Emilie Schindler became homesick for Germany after living fifty years in Argentina. However, for now, for today, I am deeply contented to live where I live and have no conscious desire to be anywhere else.

Friday, July 19, 10 a.m.

This, my dearest Helen, was supposed to get to you before you came back from the writing workshop. It didn't. No good reason; it just didn't. I am again sitting in the kitchen. Chris has gone to the chiropractor, so peace reigns. Our official invitations have finally come from St. Petersburg. All it takes now is for the staff at the embassy to do the paperwork, and then we are all set to go. Well, not true. I have a million things to organize, and I am not great at living in the future, so it's somewhat difficult for me to plan for something that is happening a month away. However, I do need to do some, as we'll be gone for a fairly long time.

Tuesday, 7 p.m.

Well, what a long, drawn-out last letter this is! My brain has written a manuscript to you in the past few days, but none of it got put on paper. Yesterday was a washout. That humidity drives me nuts. We have air conditioning, but I feel so confined when the windows are closed. Even in the coldest days in winter, we have windows open. Now I am sitting in the kitchen, a gentle

breeze blowing through the patio doors, the sound of tennis balls, children playing, our wind chimes ringing softly; sheer, utter bliss.

Our tennis playing is on hold as Chris has hurt his back. I certainly miss it, but I had a great long, quick walk today and I dance around the house to jazz music. I just can't sit and listen to it; I have to move. We delivered the visa stuff to the embassy, so it all should be ready by August 6. I am having more trouble with Canadian bureaucracy than with the Russians. Before they can process my OAS[41] forms, they need my landed immigrant proof! That was in my passport in 1968. Well, I ain't got that passport anymore. I have my Canadian citizenship, my CPP, which I paid into from 1971, and I also received child benefits. But no, not enough. I guess I'll never be accepted as a true Canadian. They need documentation, so I went twice to the Citizenship and Immigration office. First time they weren't open (they are only there between 10 a.m. and 1 p.m.); the second time I was told that since September 11, I could only get the forms by phone; security and all that. It took me half a day to get a live person on the phone. I will have the form in three weeks and will have to pay $35. What a fucking rip-off! I am so very lucky, Helen, that I don't have to deal with these people very often. I don't know how those immigrants who don't speak either official language cope. There were people sitting on the floor at the Citizenship and Immigration office, waiting in the hallway, not one chair in sight. Had lunch with Joan Wilcox today. So we both had a good old moan, and now I'm moaning again, oh, well.

[41] Old Age Security

I am very excited at finding the Attic Press in Ireland. Their criteria seem so perfect for our letters. So my hope is high that they will receive us well. I am as satisfied as I will get about my choice of letters to send. Biography is difficult for me. I think I come across so scattered; maybe not scattered, but certainly a "Jill of all trades and mistress of none." Mind you, one of the ancient Greeks said that "everyone should play the flute, but only just, if they wanted to be a complete human being"! I'll try to write something up before Friday, and maybe you will have some suggestions to make.

Darling Helen, I can't tell you how grateful I am that you responded to my suggestion of our writing to each other, and I am so terribly impressed with the two of us for staying with it throughout the year. How easy it would have been for one of us to grow tired of it all. That will tell you how right it was for the pair of us.

Well done, Helen and Oonagh! Sounds like a Mother Superior, eh?

I can't imagine writing to anyone else from this kitchen. Somehow it brings you closer, and I find it easier to write, and all of a sudden I am feeling very sad, Helen, that our project has come to an end. No wonder I kept postponing finishing this letter. Still, there will be Russia. I just hope there will be a welcoming spot for me to write to you from. It can't be just any old where; it has to have soul.

So my dearest friend, with my love, admiration and total gratitude,

Oonagh

Acknowledgments

We wrote these letters for the joy of it. We loved the notion of two women friends turning the world of instant messaging on its head, and reclaiming the old-fashioned thrill and discipline of putting pen to paper. But we also dreamed that some day our letters might be read by others. That dream was both exciting and dangerous, because honesty is exciting and dangerous. If the letters were published, who would celebrate? Who would understand? Who would pay a price?

We still have all those questions. But in the end, we decided the risk was worth taking. If feminists won't at least try to tell it like it is, who will? We know that letters are like snapshots. They are of the moment, of when a letter was written. They reveal truths, but not absolute ones. From day to day, our feelings and thoughts changed, and so did we.

There's nothing resembling "balance" in the letters; things are left out, and some parts of our lives receive more attention than others. There are plenty of contradictions, and, since we have no choice, we embrace them all.

To the people who gave us the room, the support, and the courage to go forward with this book, we offer our heartfelt thanks.

The women of Second Story Press—Margie Wolfe and Laura McCurdy in particular—brought tremendous skill and warmth to a complicated process.

Our deepest gratitude to Judy Field. Without her incredible computer and organizational skills, without her personal warmth and generosity, our letters would not have become a manuscript.

Helen very much appreciates Gil Levine for his refreshing openness in being written about in the letters, for his unwavering support of her involvement in this project, and for being the one man with whom she can be the person she truly is, warts and all.

Oonagh expresses her heartfelt thanks to Christopher Levenson for his loving support throughout the writing and editing of these letters. His patience, sense of humour, and belief in her writing abilities sustained her through her many periods of self-doubt.

Helen and Oonagh